Finding Divine Flow

An Entrepreneurial Journey

By Camelle Daley

First Edition Paperback November 2019

PO Box 5897
Milton Keynes
MK10 1FL
United Kingdom

www.FindingDivineFlow.com

ISBN: 978-1-9162513-0-4 paperback
       978-1-9162513-1-1 ebook
       978-1-9162513-2-8 audiobook

DEDICATION

Dedicated to my Mum and Dad who paved the way.
To my husband Peter Daley who supports me all the way
and my daughters Mya and Amelia-Rae who are following
as I lead the way.

.

In loving memory of

My Dad, my greatest encourager and teacher who would
be beaming at the launch of this book.
Mum & Dad Daley for being a practical,
real life example of love, prayer and laughter.
My beautiful Auntie Joy whose memory and name remind
me to smile and live life to the full.
My precious Uncle Dolvin, my dad's best friend. Thank
you for always believing in me and pushing me.
My clever, funny cousin Jason, such an
amazing soul. We miss you all dearly.

FOREWORD

To the Christian Creative ready to launch their dream, reading this page-turner you can only be inspired. Camelle shares the highs and lows of her journey with a heart to give, help and inspire.

To see this Preachers Kid go from strength to strength has been a joy. I remember the teenage Camelle on our ministry team to Cape Town South Africa operating in joy and excellence.

As God poured into Camelle and she poured out into this book, may God pour into you and fill you up to overflow into others.

Bishop Wayne Malcolm
The Business Bishop

FOREWORD

CAMELLE DALEY is a Phenomenal Global Fashion Designer for Women in Ministry. From the onset of her birth up until now... her ability to Design Fashion for Women in Ministry has evolved and continues to evolve from day-to-day!

Her ability to transport a Design from Heaven into manifestation on Earth is remarkable and noteworthy. I am grateful to be one of the recipients of her professional Clergy Attire at its early stages. Ten years of doing what she loves is nothing compared to the lifetime of the creativity that shall come from her Dreams that haven't been dreamed yet!

Reading this book, will answer your "How did She do That" questions. But, I'd like to take this opportunity to Speak to her Future and Declare that Her Creative Abilities will Manifest Beyond the confines of this Book and Launch her into Dimensions of Clergy Fashion Designs for Women in Ministry that will soon be seen in Global Magazines!

This book gives a brief scenario of her past and present journey towards Greater Greatness. Have fun gleaning from inside the creative mind of CAMELLE DALEY!

Chanda London Ministries
Los Angeles, California; USA

CONTENTS

ACKNOWLEDGMENTS

I want to thank God who has been my forever-best friend and guiding light throughout my entire life. His word is the lamp that shows me where my feet are now and it's also the light that shines on the path ahead of me.

I am grateful for the all the Bishops, Pastors and teachers that have poured into my life from my granddad Crossgell and Elder Watt to Pastor Winston Carnegie and my forever covering Pastor's (and Uncle and Auntie) Winston and Christine Carter. Thank you for investing seeds of the word of God in me. May you reap a hundredfold.

Lilly for your excellent and careful editing. Jeanette for reading my early scripts. Sisters; Marie for cover design and Kimberley for my photo. Bishop Malcolm and Evangelist Chanda London for my incredible foreword.

My hubby, Peter Daley, my love, proof-reader, audiobook recorder and biggest supporter. My girls for your expectant eyes and innocent hearts that keep me accountable to keep showing up at home and at work.

Sisters, brother, amazing in-laws, aunties, uncles and cousins, I love you for your contribution to who I have become.

My small, precious and powerful circle of friends who I call queens and sister-friends; you know who you are. You show up for me and I for you.

To every client who has purchased my products, commented on, shared or liked a post; you are the reason I have this story to tell, it truly is an honour to serve you.
Forever Grateful!

Introduction

This is an account of how my conversations with God led me to my dream role, job and business.

It tells the stories and lessons I have learnt as a God-loving wife, mum and entrepreneur – how I am discovering my purpose and pursuing it whilst balancing life with God's help and guidance.

****

I have built a successful business and the scripture verse below really resonates with me:

'He told them another parable.
"The kingdom of heaven is like leaven (yeast)
*that **a woman** took and hid in three measures of flour,*
till it was all leavened (raised).'
(Matthew 13:33 ESV)

I feel like this woman. All I am is basic flour, an ingredient. On its own, nothing much. Some people see me as raised up, successful and doing well, but what is hidden in my story (in my flour) is a little yeast (the kingdom of Heaven). When the yeast is mixed in with the flour, after a while it's hard to define the flour from the yeast. You can't see the yeast but you can see its effects. This is me; you can't see my prayers, my relationship with God and my devotion to Him but you can see the effects of His presence in my life and business.

I am "that friend". When my friends come to me for advice I'll give them a little, but the essence of my

advice will be:
"pray on it"
"give it to God"
"let Him lead you"
"He knows the detail of the detail and has the perfect solution, I don't."
Yes, I'm "that friend", because I truly believe God knows! And when we trust Him and love Him, He makes all things work together for our good.

I want to help Christian creatives launch their dreams! I am a creative Christian, I saw a need I could fulfil creatively and succeeded. I don't have all of your answers but I hope something in my story will inspire you and point you in the right direction. My prayer is that that direction is God!

Disclaimer: This book was written from the heart of a worshipper of God. I have a relationship with God that I share in these pages. You will be challenged as you read and you will encounter God's kindness and His love for you.

Camelle Daley

Chapter 1
Journey to finding Purpose

Early one cloudy English morning in March around 5:30am, I am sitting at my kitchen table, reflecting on my journey to this very moment. I am preparing to give a talk at a local community event in Milton Keynes. And, as I reflect, there's a theme forming - fashion, marketing, business, purpose and ministry.

I didn't know I would end up running a fashion label and catering for women in ministry around the world - and I get to do marketing every day. I mean, you can't make this stuff up! My younger self would be so excited about this future.

From my early encounters with the Honourable Bishop Norman L Wagner, I learnt that God created me for a purpose. I pursued God like crazy. Constantly asking God, "Show me my purpose". I've just been hungry for it. I enjoy knowing more and more of myself and understanding my various strengths and abilities.

I am God's creation and He has crafted an incredible cocktail of all the things I am, from past generations to present successes and mistakes. He pulled all of that together into the person called Camelle ilona Daley. There are some things that only I can do the way I do them.

In this book I want you to realise, you too are a perfect combination and cocktail of all the things from past generations to present successes and mistakes. He pulled all of that together into the person called (insert your name here). There are some things that only you can do the way you do them.

God created you as a
gift to the world.

Finding the patterns and themes

I always loved hair and **fashion**. I worked as a hairdresser part time during school and I studied Textiles in high school. I enjoyed Textiles but it was so laborious, we took a whole school year to make one simple shift dress. It was so frustrating because I wanted to do more. A precious family friend, Biola, took me under her wing and in six weeks taught me step by step and I made a fully lined, fully interfaced two-piece suit (I wore that tailored black suit out, lol). There was a lot of unpicking but what I learnt was invaluable.

I have a love for **business**, my dad had his own painting and decorating business. My uncles and older cousins had businesses too. I was used to designing my Dad's letterheads and typing up his estimates. I watched him at the dining table crunch the numbers with pen, paper and no calculator.

So, when it was time to go to college I wanted to do a **business** course but thought, at that time, I would find a straight business course boring. So, I enrolled at the London College of Fashion to study "The Business of Fashion". This was such a great fit for my creative business mind. I learnt about business but everything had a fashion angle and I loved it. Following that I studied more Fashion Business with a **Fashion Management Consultant** and industry insider, David Jones. He is a seasoned Fashion Business Consultant who is recognised for his many years of contribution to the Fashion Industry. I still have the privilege of meeting with him regularly to discuss and develop my fashion brand.

My hope here is that if I show you my story, themes and roots, you'll begin to see your own. Where do you find pleasure and what causes you pain? These are patterns and themes pointing to your purpose.

A life-changing, life-altering event:

In October 2008 I went to visit my Dad at his home in Croydon. He hadn't been well for a while, and was having tests done, but didn't seem to be getting better. He was sitting at the head of the dining table in his conservatory that he loved.

"Take down that picture and read the back", he said. I took it down and it read: *'first mention of the big c May 2008'*. My heart sank! I didn't know, he couldn't bring himself to even say the word to me; he just let me read it.

In his day, my Dad was a preacher, and he was always preaching to us - telling us that, "All things work together for good in the end, no matter how bad things get". He was a tower of strength to the entire family and to me. The eldest of seven, he was the life and soul of every party. He had quick wit, an air of joy around him at all times and a depth of wisdom when he spoke. He was captivating.

I didn't know that would be one of the last times I would get to see him, speak to him and kiss his forehead.

That was a tough season in my life; trying to do life without Dad's presence. I'd see something on TV and grab my phone to tell him to turn it over and then remembered that I couldn't. He loved to laugh. He was impressed with people who got paid to have fun, to make people laugh and do work they enjoyed.

He loved his creative painting and decorating work and he was excellent at his craft and very fast. When his clients would come home to see all the work he had done in just one day, they would ask if it was just him? "There were three of us," he would say. The client would stop looking shocked and smile. Then he continued, "Me, myself and I." Everyone would laugh and he would get a ton of referrals because everyone loved him.

Life after Dad was a very reflective time for me. One day I was thinking about my middle name that he gave me. It's ilona. I googled it and found out it was Hungarian for 'Beauty'. I suddenly fell in love with the name. The name that most people couldn't pronounce properly, now had a deeper meaning and personal connection.

Then the next day, in the shower, I heard in my spirit: *"House of ilona, House of beauty, for earthly and spiritual royalty!"*

I knew it was time for me to start my own fashion label. The House of ilona was born.

The Clergy Collection

My big sister, graphic designer Marie, created my

logo for me. I built a website, set up my business as a sole trader, had my logo printed onto clothing labels and I was ready to design and make my first collection.

I showed my very first collection at Chelsea Fashion Week, in London. It was an incredible experience. My collection had great reviews and the requests began to pour in to do other Fashion Weeks and magazine shoots around the world.

I was excited about the birth of this business and I was even more excited about the birth of my first baby. Yes, I was five months pregnant with our first child at that first show. I didn't know what life would look like for me as a first time Mum. I struggled with severe pelvic pain during my pregnancy. Sitting and standing were incredibly painful, so I took my foot off the gas and slowed down.

After our baby girl was born, I started to get bespoke requests. I made my designs to order and designed custom pieces for my growing client base.

One day, a long-time friend of mine, Chantel, who was recently ordained as a Youth Pastor, asked for my help.

"Once a month we have to wear our clergy collar for Communion. I keep trying to get out of wearing one, but if I don't have a collar next time, I'm in trouble," she said, as she burst out into a cheeky laugh. "Camelle, I'm not wearing the ugly shirt. Can you make me a dress please?"

So I made her a simple black, A-line, knee length clergy dress. I had no idea what had just begun. I had no idea this would be the first of many thousands of clergy dresses I would design, make and eventually manufacture. I had no idea.

Chantel wore this simple little black clergy dress at the next Communion Service and everyone loved it! I was shocked. Really? She said people wanted to know where she got it from and where they could get one for the next Communion Service.

It was one of the simplest things I had made. I was intrigued. Would other Women in Ministry like a clergy dress instead of a shirt?

I put a sample picture on my website, and included the fact that they could be made to order and delivered anywhere in the world within two weeks. I had been learning about Facebook Ads at the time so I decided to put these new skills to work. After two weeks I had to take the ads down because I couldn't sew the clergy dresses fast enough. There was a demand. I found an untapped niche.

I then got samples made, pictures taken and found a manufacturer to help me produce them.

Spread wide and thin versus narrow and deep

After the birth of our baby girl, Mya, in 2010, my husband Peter and I agreed that I wouldn't go back to my full-time Council job. (Oh, by the way, I did all of the above on the side whilst working a full-time job). When we worked out the cost of childcare and the general cost of going back to work (clothes, lunch the commute etc.), it would leave me with about twenty pounds per week in my hand. Going back to work for the Council would only make sense if this was a credible career path I was working towards and wanted to keep my position. Only then would it be worth the sacrifice; this wasn't the case for me.

So, my conclusion was, if I can stay home and make at least twenty pounds per week I don't have to go back to a full-time job. It was a no brainer.

At this point, I had a 'Clergy Collection' business that was doing well, sales were steady and I had a consistent flow of clients. Over the next two years to keep the cash flow coming in - to justify me not working a full-time job – I realised that I'd have to put my other skills to use. So, I was selling the clergy dresses, working with the body shaper company, doing bespoke work for clients, building websites for people, and let's add the most beautiful thing to this - I was also pregnant with my second baby.

In 2013 I had a toddler running around, a baby on the way and I was juggling all these other things. It was too much! I had been hearing it in all the training I'd been listening to (while sewing I would listen to literally hundreds of audiobooks). There was a theme, getting louder and stronger. I needed to stop juggling, and focus.

FOCUS

I had so much going on, juggling various business activities and life. I was praying and asking God, "What do I focus on?" There wasn't an obvious choice. Everything was doing well here and there.

Then a powerful question dropped into my spirit:
"What has been the most consistent?"

That was it! Everything I was juggling read like an ECG reading - highs and lows, highs and lows. The one thing that was consistent was the 'Clergy Dresses'. They weren't high, they weren't low - they were consistent.

So I knew that's where I needed to put my energy. I believed this was the answer to my prayer. I moved in faith. I took action on the word I received.

That very day my faith was tested! I had about twenty emails from previous clients asking me to design and make bespoke items for them. This was a test of my faith because this was straight cash. Instant gratification. Some bills paid. Money in the bank. You catch my drift?

Was this a blessing of work or a distraction from purpose? I said a prayer,
"Lord, I believe this is you telling me to focus on 'Clergy Dresses', so I'm going to move by faith, turn down these opportunities and focus on what has been consistent. In Jesus name, Amen."

I then sat in my lounge, with my laptop and replied to everyone. "Unfortunately I am no longer offering bespoke services."

That was hard!

The idea of focused energy felt great though! I went to work. I went into production on over two-hundred clergy dresses and tops. I did a Clergy photo shoot and produced our first clergy catalogue, after which I sent out a press release to media and waited for the orders to roll in... And Nothing! The sound of crickets. No orders, no press hype. Nothing.

What had I done? Did I hear right?

A few weeks later on a Friday afternoon, I had the usual request for a press release and photos. I had them ready and sent them off. It was a bank holiday weekend so I didn't have to go back to work until the following Tuesday. The phone rang; it was a new client checking that her order went through okay. As I checked on her order, I asked my usual question, "How did you hear about House of ilona?" Her reply stunned me. "In the Times." I kept my best poker face and voice until she hung up and then, I SCREAMED.

That week, House of ilona was in the Times, the Telegraph, the Washington Post and the Huffington Post. I did interviews on most of the BBC radio stations and Christian radio stations. All the stock I had manufactured sold out. God did it!

What I would tell my younger self:
- Don't be in such a rush
- Enjoy the journey, don't endure it
- Stick with God, He has a perfect plan
- Something beautiful will come out of the hardest time in your life
- Don't hate your name, people can't pronounce it now but it's a gift and will be spoken around the world

Study and learn from your own history, it will connect you to your present purpose and direct you to your future destiny.

Chapter 2
Process the Process

"To really understand who you are,
where you are and where you are going;
go to the One who created you and
spend quality time alone in prayer and journaling.
An intentional journey to understanding
who you are in God is Powerful."

The passage quoted above is from my journal. I cannot count the amount of times my own words have encouraged me! Flicking back to this day a year earlier or last month or last week, my journey and the lessons I've learnt inspire ME. When I can go back and read in detail the emotion of what I was going through and how I got through it, there's nothing quite like it. I encourage you to do the same.

Purpose of journaling

It's 5:25am on another morning and I've been up a while. I've **prayed**, **read** and **meditated** on a

15

scripture from the bible and read two chapters of an inspiring book. I'm now at my kitchen table with a cup of coffee and my laptop. I am prayerfully **writing** in my electronic Journal. (It's the 'Day One' App). I'll do my daily **declarations** soon and close my eyes to ensure what I'm saying lines up with what I'm **visualising**. Then, while Peter and the girls are still sleeping I'll hit the gym by 6am for some **exercise,** in the car I'll write one to three **actions** I will do that day to take me closer to my goal. I'll be back home by 7am to get the girls up and ready for school.

Here are the seven powerful keys to a powerful daily routine as detailed in the paragraph above:

1. Prayer

Talk to God, thank Him for all the good things He has done, for all the things He's working together for your good. Pour out your heart about any issues you have, then leave room, silence, and space for God to speak to your heart.

2. Reading/Meditating

Read the Bible and a chapter or two from a good book in your field.

3. Writing

Take time to journal, process the process of life and write what you're feeling in your heart.

4. Declaring

Create powerful declarations to speak out loud every

day. Take it a step further and record yourself saying it so you can play it back to yourself too.

5. Visualize
Daydream, exercise your powerful imagination, see and visualise what you are declaring. Be specific, choose something and conceptualize it in your mind.

6. Exercise
I aim for forty-five minutes strength (weight) training three days per week. Other days I aim for ten to forty-five minutes. It's so good to keep the body moving, active and healthy, allowing the body to work up a sweat.

7. Action
Take intentional action on your goal, decision, dream, whether big or small, do something!

As I'm journaling, I'm praying, I'm writing, I'm speaking to God. I'm also speaking to myself, encouraging myself, analysing the previous day's highlights and what this season of life feels like. As I'm asking questions, I'm writing answers. I'm 'Processing the Process'. (See the author's *Finding Divine Flow Journal* to help with this.)

These daily habits help me to reconnect with myself and reconnect with God. I tap into who I am and where I am, so any broken parts in me can be healed.

Physician heal thyself and know yourself
(Luke 4:23)

A physician is a medical doctor. When you go to the doctor, what's the first thing they need to know? Your symptoms. Do you know your symptoms?

To heal yourself, you need to know yourself. Start with right now:

- Where are you?
- How are you feeling and why do you feel this way?
- What's your physical status?
- Where are you emotionally?
- Where are you mentally?
- Where are you spiritually?
- What do you intend on doing about your current situation?
- What is your motive?

God's word is a lamp to our feet and a light to our path (Psalm 119:105). A lamp is a small light. We need God's Word to shine a small, specific, targeted light to our feet.

Where am I?

This is such a powerful question. Where you are right now is linked to where you've been and where you're going. Where was Noah physically? In the middle of tonnes of gopher wood, and he had a plan from God to build something called an ark. Where was he according to the lamp of the Word? He was building the thing that would save and preserve people and animals. He was in the middle of an enormous building project that would save the world. It looked like a bunch of wood but it was world-changing.

Where are you? Does it look like a bunch of materials around you or inside of you?

Who you are and what you have are potentially world changing!

What do you have?

In 2 Kings Chapter 4, the Prophet Elisha asked the widow to analyse her current situation. He asked her, "what do you have in your house?" Her immediate answer was "... nothing ......"! Isn't it crazy how often we think that what we have is NOTHING! Who we are is NOTHING and what we have to offer is NOTHING. This is a lie from the pit.

If only you could see the treasure God has placed inside of you! It would blow your mind.

This widow went on to say "...nothing but a pot of oil". When you think about it and begin to analyse, what is your "nothing but a pot of..."?

What's that thing you have inside of you that feels so small and too insignificant to even mention?

Life and everything she held dear were slipping through her fingers, fast. She's mourning the death of her husband; he has left her with debt. A creditor has threatened to take her sons as slaves. Her boys, who are meant to be looking after her, may be ripped out of her life. She would be left with no one; she's gone from full to empty. It was too much.

She went to the prophet in utter desperation. Her husband was one of the sons of the Prophets and now she needed help from The Prophets. In faith, she followed Elisha's instruction on what to do with this little pot of oil. The woman and her sons borrowed vessels from their neighbours, as many as they could. They came in the house as instructed, shut the door as instructed and **behind those closed doors, God worked a miracle!**

That little oil multiplied. **She poured out of her pot of oil** and filled every single vessel in the house to the brim. Elisha then instructed her to sell the oil, clear her debts and live off the rest.

When you give God your little, He can do so much with it.

Notice how the flow, the increase and the overflow came from God via her own little pot of oil. God used her pot of oil.

What's your little pot of oil?

Will you give it to God to bless it, break it and distribute it?

Let's look at the day five thousand plus people came to hear Jesus preach in the park (John chapter 6). Service ran over, it was dinnertime and they were hungry, with no shops for miles. Jesus asked the disciples what they had. All they had, which seemed insignificant in this huge multitude of people, was five loaves and two fish. But Jesus took them in His hands, blessed and broke them and miraculously fed over five thousand people, until they were all full and there was food left over.

All I have is... some admin skills
All I have is... my story about what I went through
All I have is... my creativity
All I have is... whatever it is you have, recognise it, acknowledge it and give it to God to use.

> ### *Prayer*
> *God, this is what I have. It doesn't seem like much to me and I'm not sure what you can do with it but I trust you with this (name it here). I give it to you to do what you will. Use it for your Glory, God. Use this and anything else inside of me that you can use.*
> *In Jesus name,*
> *Amen*

Power Point:
Know, love and appreciate how far you've come!

I am so excited about your future. You are in such a powerful position right here and right now. I hope you see that and move forward intentionally.

You have a story to tell, a testimony to share.

There is a book in all of us. There is a book that we can write but there is also a book that has already been written.

'You saw me before I was born.
*Every day of my life was **recorded in your book**.*
Every moment was laid out before a single day had passed.'
Psalm 139:16 NLT

Sometimes the only thing stopping you from writing and telling your story is content. You build your content by documenting your journey. You document your journey by processing your process.

We cannot underestimate the power of journaling. Our memories hold vital keys to our future.

Process the Process

Every person who I have encouraged to journal has found it life-changing. When they're in the midst of a life challenge and come back to me for advice, my first question is, "Are you still journaling?" Usually they've stopped.

Having a conversation with someone who processes, journals and prays, is a higher level of conversation. They already have an understanding of where they are in life and what is happening, this is where *'iron sharpens iron'* (Proverbs 27:17).

Consider this: Who's your go-to person? When you're going through, when something's happened or is happening, who is that person? If it's not already, my prayer is for your answer to be, God.

Open your personal settings and change your default to God. After that, go wherever or to whomever, but let them be your number two. But may your default be God. Initially, as you try defaulting to God, you may find yourself praying while calling or texting your number two, but bring God in. Allow Him to be the 'legit' King of your life.

Take it to Him first and He will direct you. THIS is how you find your Divine Flow:

- Problem arises
- Go to God first
- Answers come via:
  - a tug in your heart, prompting what you should do,
  - a clear word from God or
  - the feeling of peace about it.

When you seek God first, when you set your default settings to God, He said He will add all "these things" on to you (Matthew 6:33). What are "these things"? They're the things you truly need.

TIP: God's not in a rush.

Divine flow can be a sudden movement or a real long process. Just know, if you trust Him in the process, He will make all things work together for your good (Romans 8:28). There are things you can't see that He's doing and it's only on reflection, after the situation has passed, that you see the reason for what seemed like God's delay.

The Power of your Words!

I have grown up with this and thankfully it has stuck with me. I am very mindful and cautious about the words I speak. I practice speaking life and I handle my words with care.

So, as you process your process by prayerfully journaling, follow through with intentional words that speak life into your situation:
- Don't play into modern stereotypes
- Don't look for the sympathy vote and
- Don't try to please anyone with the comfort of negativity.

> *'But let a man examine himself...'*
> 1 Corinthians 11:28 KJV

God said to examine yourself, search yourself and process. Move through the process of forgiving yourself, others and even God.

Your life and mind are a reflection of your business.

In the early days of business, I struggled with pricing my products correctly. There were nice clothes available at cheaper stores, I knew people who shopped at these places and sometimes I did too. I was concerned that people would think my prices were too high. I had a conversation with my coach at the time and she had to give me a lesson in value.

"Can people buy the type of clothes you design cheaper?" she asked.

"Yes they can," I responded.

"Then let them! People who want to buy cheap clothes know where to go. When people buy from you they're buying into the value you bring, the experience you come with, the time you take to design and source fabric and how you deliver. This isn't mass-produced. You are a designer and provide designer clothes. Know the value you bring!"

The conversation totally shifted my thinking. I've never been the same since.

> *'For as he thinketh in his heart, so is he.'*
> Proverbs 23:7

The conviction hit me. I thought, "If I don't believe my work has value, people will follow my belief. If I do believe my work has value, people will also follow my belief."

My business was a direct reflection of my thoughts. When I thought my prices were too high and no one would buy, *no one bought.* When I valued my work and believed it was worth its value, and more, *people bought.*

The Picasso story always encourages me. It goes something like this. A lady recognised the great Picasso in a restaurant and asked him to draw her picture on a napkin. He did, it took thirty seconds. He then told the lady it would cost three thousands pounds and she was shocked and asked why it cost so much when it only took him thirty seconds. His answer was, "No, not thirty seconds, it took me forty years to be able to do this."

Processing the process:

- What you do on a regular and consistent basis is who you become
- There is power in patience
- There is power in the process
- The process is the MAKING OF YOU
- The destination is where you end up but the process is the person you become, so you show up powerfully to the destination.

"I truly believe life is a beautiful jigsaw puzzle where God has the final overall picture.
No matter how messy all the pieces may look, there is a beautiful picture, waiting for you to put all the pieces together and to see what God had in store all along."

Chapter 3
Be ready to press play

It's hard to steer a stationary vehicle.
Miracles take place when you take that first step
followed by another. When you create the plan,
execute the plan and leave room for God to edit.

Back in 2013 I remember praying so hard for the
money and resources I needed to really build my
business. I had many ideas and was desperate for
God's help to make this a reality. I would be asking
God for a specific amount of money regularly and
consistently. Every time the thought crossed my
mind I would turn it into a prayer. Yes, I could write
a business plan, get a business loan - I've been taught
this method for years. Instead, I wanted to prove God
in business so I turned to Him instead.

Every time the thought crossed my
mind I would turn it into a prayer.

Then I heard in my spirit: "...be ready to press play!"

I instantly knew exactly what this meant for me.

Yes, I was praying, but if God dropped all the money and resources I was asking for into my lap, would I be ready for it? My honest answer was no! If God gave me everything I was asking for in that moment, I would then be running around, trying to bring it all together. I wasn't ready for the very thing I was asking for.

Here's what I did next. I got busy. I started doing everything I needed to do. Pulling together everything I could - information, contacts, designs and ideas. As I did this, the things I did and didn't need became clear. All the resources I needed began to come together and fall into place.

Be ready to press play

I was in the gym listening to some marketing training and the trainer said "....about five or six years ago, people everywhere started to use the words *'press play'* in their marketing." I thought, "That's so cool, that's the same word God gave me in that season." Maybe it was in the atmosphere.

My encouragement to you today is, "Be ready to press play." God has the desires of your heart and the answers to all your prayers.

The questions to consider are:

- Are you ready for it?
- Have you done your part?
- Are your heart, mind, body and environment ready to receive the fullness of what you're asking for?

My miracle car

I was eighteen and believing God for my first car. I really needed one but didn't have enough money. By faith, I started a car corner in my bedroom. There, I placed all the little things I wanted for my car. The little air freshener, the A to Z street atlas (remember those), my de-icer, window wiper and cassette tapes I had recorded. (You can probably tell I'm going back a few years). I was excited and ready for my blessing and it came in a big beautiful way.

At the time I was working at the head office of a store in their Marketing department. It was a twenty-minute walk from home through a very unsafe area, but it was the only walking route between my home and work. Every other week we would hear of women getting raped and all sorts of terrible things happening there. Whenever I walked that route I would be walking and praying heaven down in my heart: *"Yea, though I walk through the valley of the shadow of death, I will fear no evil: for thou art with me; thy rod and thy staff they comfort me."* (Psalm 23:4) I would walk and pray until I could see my office building in view and knew I was back in safe territory.

I didn't just want a car; I needed a car or a new job. My dad would sometimes lend me his, but he needed it most days to transport his painting and decorating work tools.

A few weeks later at the New Year's Eve service at my church, the clock had struck midnight, everyone was hugging and praying for each other. A lady from my church came over and hugged me. She said, "God wants you to be safe and He doesn't want you to walk anymore." I was rocked to my core, it still brings tears of joy to my eyes thinking about it. Not many people knew about this terrifying walk I had to do each day. So when she said these words, I knew it was **straight from God's heart to mine**. He spoke directly to the essence of how I was feeling and said He wanted me to be safe and not walk any more. How kind!

I was filled with love. I was so happy, so full; I was done. But she hadn't finished speaking. She went on, "Go and choose a car tomorrow and I will pay for it!"

Not only did God see me and speak to my heart, He also made provision. I was in tears and so grateful to God and this precious lady. Exactly what I needed. JUST WOW!

It doesn't finish here! I didn't speak much to this lady again that day. The next day after work, I walked straight to the Volkswagen showroom. I spoke to a car salesman and he wanted to show me a Polo that didn't have much miles, it was only used as a courtesy car. It was dark and raining outside but he brought the car around. It was dark green - not a colour I would have chosen. I sat inside, it was really dark. THEN he switched the car lights on and all the lights on the dashboard turned electric blue, my heart skipped a beat. It was beautiful (most dashboard colours were green back then). It was also the same colour my mobile phone was when I switched it on. It just felt right. I said, "I'll take it". Just like that.

I didn't negotiate, I didn't have anyone come over to check it out for me. I just knew this was my car.

We went inside and he took a non-refundable deposit from me - a cheque that would clear out my bank account. I had gone to the showroom, I had paid a deposit, all on a word! Can I add, the lady who gave me the word at church didn't even tell me how much she could afford. I didn't know if it was seven hundred pounds or seven thousand pounds. I just paid a non-refundable deposit on a car I had seen and fallen in love with, because of the dashboard lights!!

A few days later I saw the lady from my church again. She asked excitedly, "Have you found a car?"

"Yes," I said hesitantly, "But I don't know what price range I should be looking at."

She responded, "I didn't ask that. I asked, have you found a car?"

When I told her the price of the car she couldn't believe her ears. She had received an inheritance and knew she was to tithe ten percent to the church but also felt she was to give the same ten percent amount to me for a car. It was the EXACT amount I needed to clear the entire balance for the car.

To this day, this is one of my favourite miracles to testify about. **God is in the detail of the detail.** He saw me, He heard me and He answered me perfectly. I love to share this story and all the steps of faith along the way. God sees us, loves us and is so faithful.

I drove that car up and down the country. Gave many people lifts to youth meetings, choir rehearsals and conferences. I had numerous counselling and coaching sessions in that car, where I would pray for and pour into people; it was a blessing to many. In this car, I drove my Mum and myself to prayer meetings and church services every week for six years. Then when I got married I said to my husband Peter, "We can sell this car now and get something bigger or we can drive it into the ground" (not the best terminology but that's what I said). We chose the latter. By the time we went to upgrade that car a few years later the passenger door couldn't open, and there were lots of little problems, but it was a great down payment for our next vehicle.

What a blessing that car was to me and so many other people. I'm even writing about it in my first book (smile).

How was I ready to press play?

I was ready, down to the tapes I had recorded and my A to Z. I wanted my blessing and I made sure I was ready for it.

We feel like we're waiting on God but He is waiting on us.

Our wedding miracle

When Peter and I were thinking about getting married, timing-wise, I wanted to have all the money together, then set the date. A wise married friend of ours said, "If we wait until we have all the money we'll probably be very old. Just go for it, you'll find ways to cut the costs, people will come out of the wood work to help and the money will come." That is exactly what happened! We set the date before we had all the money, people helped, we worked more jobs, we figured out where we wanted to spend the bulk of our money; our rings, honeymoon and house.

Everything else we set within a tight budget.

Peter proposed in January and we were married in June of the same year. I walked down the aisle and that day in June 2005 my husband-to-be and I didn't owe a penny. Everything was paid for. With God's help, we did it.

How was I ready to press play?

- First, we had many confirmations from God that we were supposed to be together
- We were ready to get married and the only thing stopping us was money
- We got engaged, trusted God, were intentional and things just began to happen.

Testing the waters – fashion sales

When I first started my fashion label I didn't have a manufacturer. I wanted one, but instead what I got was a great piece of business advice from my business coach. This advice was worth thousands of pounds and hundreds of hours. She said (not to me directly, it was a post on her huge Facebook Page but I took it personally) *"grow organically, don't invest loads of money if you've not confirmed the demand through sales".*

I needed to - Follow what people buy not just what they say.

I had received great feedback on my Facebook pages about my designs, so I wanted to manufacture them. From this advice I chose to make-to-order instead of going into production with a manufacturer. Unfortunately, once I was open for business, all these Facebook "likes" didn't translate into sales. I was relieved I didn't invest in manufacturing. Making-to-order made it much easier to follow the demand and make changes quickly.

When your business is small you can be quick, agile and respond to your market. Don't despise the small start, small is powerful.

What CAN you do now?

As a Fashion Designer, I have designs coming out of me all … of … the … time. But my brand isn't about me just producing the hundreds of designs in my heart and head. Instead, it's a narrow range of quite similar designs that are tweaked but based on the same sort of style.

I've followed the demands of my clients who have asked for more of the same designs, but in additional colours. I could go into production with a load of my design ideas but these are not tested. Producing what people are asking and paying for is where the profitability is.

Other brands have based their business model on bringing new styles out every four to six weeks. It comes in, sells out, then the new ones come. If you blink you miss it, you won't see it again - it creates demand.

I love this model, but it's not how the demand was organically created for my business. My clients want a uniformed look for their ministry wear. They want to come back each year to replace what they have, when they have an event such as wedding, funeral, convention or a speaking engagement. They know what they're going to get when they come to the House of ilona.

I have followed the demand, created what the majority of people were asking for, served consistently, developed relationships and built our following.

Key takeaways:

- Are you ready for what you're praying for?
- What do you need to do to be ready?
- Make a list and get to work.

*When we take action on what
we're believing, our faith is activated.
We need to mix our faith with
action to activate the miracle.*

Chapter 4
It takes courage

Courage to build my team

So far, the ten years of building House of ilona have taken some courageous steps, some optional, most were mandatory. From building my team to outsourcing things like product fulfilment. Looking to the future, I could easily keep things as they are but I feel the tug to build, write, coach and speak. It takes courage to dare to break new ground! I pray this chapter encourages you to be courageous.

In the early days of business, I would hire freelancers to help me with business administration and some marketing. I'd get a friend to help with my stocktakes when I was working from home. I had a really bad experience with a freelancer, who, at the end of our time working together, created her own email account in my business name in order to offer a response for a job reference pertaining to a position she was seeking. I was concerned we had been hacked. I asked her and she denied it at first and then eventually confessed. It was so hard, I felt betrayed, exposed, and I knew it would be hard for me to trust someone in and with my business again.

I prayed that God would heal my heart. I got speaking to a good friend about it all and it was so helpful to share and just pour out my heart, as I could feel myself not wanting to ever hire anyone again. She allowed me to vent and later on mentioned in passing, that she was going to get a part-time job for some extra cash. I offered her a job on the spot. Like falling off a horse, I needed to get back on again, otherwise I'm not sure I would have. She was also a Christian and my first part-time employee, and it worked great. She also ran a side business, so our entrepreneurial minds, mixed with regular prayer, were an incredible combination. Before we knew it, she was working full-time and her sister came on board part-time.

It was great that so much work could get done. It was such pressure to now manage staff, workload and ensure everyone got paid on time. Some months were easier than others but it was an incredible achievement and a courageous step.

Courage to outsource

I remember in 2005 going to Bishop Wagner's PIP (Pentecost in Perspective) Conference. At the end of one of the services a lady prayed for me and prophesied that she could see me in a building, sewing clothing for the men and women of God. She didn't know I was a fashion designer, (I was doing it very part time at that point) and I hadn't started the clergy line yet.

Around seven years later, I was in the sewing room in my home, sewing a man's clergy robe someone had ordered and I was sewing clergy dress after clergy dress. That word suddenly came back to me and I burst into tears because this is exactly what I was doing.

I remember spending all day marketing the business, doing social media and handling client care queries. It was a good day, but I was exhausted. I then needed to spend the next couple hours sewing the orders I had just generated. I sat at my sewing machine, in position, but with my eyes closed. It was too much. I was exhausted and something had to give.

After a long search, I found a manufacturer. Sending that first order as well as the money was nerve racking. Everything proceeded seamlessly and for the very first time, I was holding in my hand, a dress I designed but didn't make. My sewing and finishing were good but theirs were on another level. I was excited about the future possibilities.

We have had thousands of our designs manufactured

and our manufacturers are a large part of my team.

Website

In early 2010 I was heavily pregnant with our first child and went from creating free websites on simple online software, to, at the time, being trained to build websites in Wordpress and understanding the search engine optimisation (SEO) that went along with it. I finally found a Wordpress theme I loved and used it for a few years. When I ran into a few problems and my previous training needed updating, I reached out to the Wordpress team for support for that particular theme and connected with Liz, who has now become my website technical support and a vital member of my team.

Fulfilment

I used to pick, pack and ship every order myself, then our staff did, and we finally outsourced to a local fulfilment company who; stock, pick, pack, ship and handle returns. When the business was run from my home, I knew about fulfilment companies but was not ready to hand my products over. After moving to our office and having staff handle the fulfilment side of the business, I was already one step removed from the process, so it was the next natural progression and when it happened, it felt right.

Courage in the face of fears

'A double minded man is unstable in all his ways.'
James 1:8

I take that to mean that a single-minded man is stable in all his ways.

I love Sarah Jakes-Robert's prayer before she preaches "...Lord remove all nerves..." Simple truth right there. I love the small, real prayers - "Lord I believe but help my unbelief..."

Prayer
I acknowledge there's some fear here, nerves and doubt, but I put that in your hands and I take on courage. Lord you said, 'the righteous are as bold as a lion' (Proverbs 28:1) so I stand in you and I do!
In Jesus name,
Amen

Then, go do what it is you need to do.

'For God hath not given us the spirit of fear;
but of power, and of love, and of a sound mind.'
2 Timothy 1:7

Not operating in the spirit of fear (doing it afraid) but doing it in the knowledge that you've given the fear, doubt and nerves to God and you stand in Him and He has wrapped you in boldness, courage and strength. This is what it means to stand in His strength and not your own.

'Let the weak say, I am strong.'
Joel 3:10

You say it, He will do the rest.

What about in areas where you are confident? Excellent, this is great. Excel here but don't get it twisted. Let's acknowledge God in all we do so that He will direct our paths. Have you ever had a knock back in your place of confidence? It can happen. If God is the God of your life, then allow Him to be the God of your weaknesses AND YOUR STRENGTHS!

I had to face the fear of being seen on social media. I have a purpose for being seen – it is to help Christian creatives launch their dreams, show them I'm doing it through the highs and lows. The more I showed up, the more I prayed and processed. I began to realise there were a handful of people I felt intimidated by. Then I realized those same people were inspired by ME! That fear was **f**alse **e**vidence **a**ppearing **r**eal (**FEAR**).

'Only be strong and courageous.'
Joshua 1:8

Courage for when the plan seemingly fails

The day came when I thought it was all over. I had my clergy line going for a while and things were really taking off. I then found a company offering similar products, they were UK based, doing market research, had feedback from hundreds of clergywomen and were about to launch their new line.

I remember reading all the comments and I went and sat on the ottoman in my hallway for around twenty minutes, but it felt like three hours. Thoughts were spinning in my head like, "it's over, I've had a really good run, I enjoyed it while it lasted, what will I do now?"

As my thoughts shifted from desperation to prayer, I thought of Oprah and that video where she speaks of her early days of having a daytime chat show. Suddenly, lots of other talk shows began to pop up. Rather than worry about that and what they were doing, Oprah decided to focus on what she was doing. By the time she looked up again, most were gone or began to niche in other areas.

That is exactly what happened for me. I decided to focus on my work, my incredible clients and future production. It worked! A few years later I looked up again and these companies were gone or began to niche into complementary areas.

Courage at breaking point

After years of growth, the business hit a dip. Our weekly numbers were the lowest they had been in years and I wondered if it was time to shut up shop. I was going to be placing a new production order with our manufacturer but hadn't yet. I actually prayed, "Lord, if you want me to shut down this business now is the time to do it; stock is low, I can sell through what's left and not place this new production order. It's the perfect time to shut things down if that's your will." I prayed hard, it's not what I wanted to do but I also had to be wise. I needed a sign.

That afternoon I had the honour of having lunch with an evangelist from California. We had a great time and I shared some of what I was going through. She said before she came to the UK, the word she woke up with that morning was "FORWARD". She was not sure what it meant or who it was for but I took it as a sign to keep going. I knew I had more designs in me, more dresses and suits to produce, which meant I had to continue with my business to see these new ideas come to pass.

Courage to get from the cross to the crown

There were three major times when I almost quit and there were also various other rocky moments. However, I learnt that the cross is HARD, but that breaking made me. That breaking is the crushing that causes my business anointing to be so rich. Finally, that breaking makes me able to face certain business challenges easier now than five to ten years ago.

Next courageous steps

Now that I have outsourced the production of the garments, the website, the picking, packing and shipping, it's left me with running the business, marketing and customer service which are currently quite manageable. In fact, it's freed up my time. As a result, I've being asked to share my story and speak more on business, fashion, styling and balancing life as an entrepreneur, wife and mum. All the speaking has led me to write this book, which has developed into coaching programmes and journals.

Recently a client replied to an encouraging email I sent out to our clergy list and she called me "an instrument of encouragement!" Those words blessed me so much!! That's exactly what I want to be and to be known as. I want to spend my time designing, connecting with and encouraging people. This brings me so much joy.

And it's with this sense of joy that I take delight in sharing this transformational story from my younger sister, Kimberley, in her own words:

*****

Story Time

Philippians 4:13 tells me that 'I can do all things through Christ which strengtheneth me.'

If I could sum up what Camelle has done for me, it would have to point to this scripture. She reminded me that I can do all things and continues to remind me each and every time I doubt.

I sat in my front room with Camelle one evening in August and I just talked. I was desperately unhappy with my employment situation. Having handed in my resignation as a teacher and facing the prospect of signing up to a supply teaching agency as a supply teacher (something I had done previously and disliked immensely). I had created a box for myself and I was stuck. My conversation with Camelle was just a moan. This was life. I didn't like it. All I wanted to do was sit and complain then I'd just live it.

In the midst of my moan, Cam heard my cry. She felt my pain. Suddenly I was stopped in my tracks. Camelle reminded me that this was just one of a multitude of options I had. It filled me with the confidence that I could do all things through Christ.

Further into this conversation I was opening

my heart and revealing my life-long passion for photography. More talk exposed all the barriers that I had created to stop myself achieving my passion - all the things I didn't have, such as the resources, money, to name just a few. Camelle took that half empty glass I was nursing and showed me how full it was. She used 4 to help me see what I did have and how if I allowed God, He could bless my 'little' abundantly. Before I knew it, our conversation was over and I had a to-do list to start my very own business.

Roll on seven months and I'm now living my dream. I'm working as a self-employed photographer and I love every minute.

This is all because Camelle Daley, my beautiful sister, took time out to really listen to me. She heard the words I spoke but also the cry of my heart beneath my words.

Camelle initiated a shift in me mentally and physically. Now I've shifted, she's with me every step of the way to keep me moving in the right direction, reminding me always to put God first.

Kimberley Lawson, Sister,
Photographer, Kica Photography
Instagram; @kica_photography

I love Kimberley's story, it's one of courage! Notice she said the talking exposed the barriers she put in her own way to stop herself achieving her passion. I could speak to her and see the barriers because I've been there. The steps we took were transformational. There was:

1) a conversation
2) on-going accountability. This was key! This is where we seek the Master's Mind and take action.

Coaching with Camelle

Following on from this book I will produce an online Finding Divine Coaching Program for serious Creatives ready to launch their dreams. You will find more details of this in the Appendix, at the end of this book.

Chapter 5
The Inevitable Effect

When people don't like the size of your dream

Have you ever met a group of people for the first time and some of them love you and some of them can't stand you? Why? Because you are You. Because you are blessed.

The same things that cause one to love you, another hates you for it

You just dream too big and the blessing is upon you. It's not the brand of clothing you're wearing, but it's something about the contentment on your face and joy in your smile that comes from your soul.

Someone looks at you and thinks *"you are blessed, happy and content, I am not. I want what you have and I don't like you because you have it. What can I do to make you feel bad, because making you feel bad will make me feel better, I think!"* This thought can happen in a split second, in the blink of an eye - in the very first impression.

The Joseph effect

Joseph was a dreamer. Not the airy-fairy type dreamer; his dreams came from God! (See Genesis chapters 37-45).

His father, Jacob, made him a coat of many colours. The only boy in his family with a coat like this, and it was from his father. The coat made him stand out from the rest. It was a visible symbol of his father's favour. He was the favourite and everyone knew it, but he didn't choose it.

God gave him dreams. These dreams were signs of what was to come in the future. It was a message from Heaven. Joseph shared his dreams with his family, but the dreams had different effects on the father and on the brothers. Whereas the dreams made Jacob think and consider, the same dreams made Joseph's eleven brothers hate him and want to do him harm.

But Joseph did not let his father's or his brother's responses stop him from sharing his dreams.

Have you ever shared a dream, goal, desire, or

decision that caused people to doubt, question or even hate you for your dream and your words? Maybe you have chosen to lose weight and have actually started to get results. It can make your friends and relatives who are struggling in this area resent your efforts, speak against you or even set traps to sabotage you.

Favour followed Joseph, coat or not

They took off Joseph's colourful coat of favour, but favour still followed him everywhere! The brothers wanted to kill Joseph but big brother Judah spared his life. Was it guilt, greed, or a mixture? Instead of killing Joseph they sold him to make some money. *Sold by his own family.*

The **favour** on Joseph's life was the linking theme that brought all the parts of the puzzle together:

- **Favour** in the form of dreams from God led his brothers to hate him so much that they put him in the pit, sold him, lied to their father and broke their father's heart
- **Favour** in the form of God causing *all Joseph did to prosper* - opened the door for him to become overseer over Potiphar's entire house
- **Favour** in the form of his status in Potiphar's house caused Potiphar's wife to become very attracted to Joseph and *she wanted some of him* and was willing to lie about him when she didn't get what she wanted

- **Favour** meant that Joseph wasn't killed for his alleged actions, he wasn't even put into regular prison. He was placed in the prison where the king's prisoners were bound, a place he could make favoured connections
- **Favour** in the form of God being with Joseph showing him mercy and giving him favour in the sight of the keeper of the prison, caused the prison keeper to put Joseph in charge of all the prisoners
- **Favour** in the form of Joseph's gift of dream interpretation caused him to eventually be released from prison to interpret the Pharaoh's dream. He was then made ruler and led Egypt through a terrible famine that caused Egypt to prosper.

In the end, Joseph's dream came to pass. Eventually, his brothers came to Egypt, bowing down to Joseph who fed them and gave them land. The result was that the twelve tribes of Israel were preserved because of the **Favour** that followed Joseph's life.

- Can you see God's favour on your life?
- Can you see a colourful thread that has weaved its way through the scenes of your life?
- What are you loved for? What are you hated for?

- Do doors seem to open and close for no logical reason but you are able to look back and see a bigger picture?
- Is someone elevating you and that same person pulling you down?
- Are people being attracted to your position?
- Are you finding favour at rock-bottom?

The Esther effect - A beautiful purpose

The story of Esther describes the journey of a young beautiful girl, chosen to be Queen and ends up risking her life to save her people. But let's dig a little deeper, below the surface, to see what that might have looked like for her socially.

She was beautiful! I'm talking jaw dropping, stand out, Beautiful! I'm sure that from a young age, her beauty would have made people notice her. Her beauty is not something she did. It's who she was and I'm sure she would get attention from boys and men which may have made her girlfriends jealous and caused her to be ostracised.

She stood out. She was used to standing out. I wonder at the level of her self-esteem as a young girl. Was it high? Did she walk in confidence or was it on the low side? Did she crave to fit in?

I'm sure whenever anyone met her for the first time, they would comment on how beautiful she was.

Maybe she was also really smart, but the first (and maybe the only) thing people saw was her beauty.

I'm sure her friends had other gifts and talents they were recognised for, such as weaving, sewing, apothecary or playing an instrument. But everyone knew what Esther was known for. I bet she wondered, "Could God ever use my beauty? I wish I had a more significant gift like…"

When they ran the Miss Babylon Pageant I can just imagine everyone pushing Esther forward as the obvious choice. Esther got to spend months being royally pampered. This pampering was an intense, full-time job, which probably meant, no time for hanging out with friends, now that she was in the running to be Queen.

A Spa Day is lovely! I highly recommend it. Maybe even a Spa Weekend but a Spa week or month and I'm bored. I'm sure Esther would have loved to have a break and just hang with her girls, but this wasn't possible for the level she was now being elevated to.

Everyone needs someone. For Esther, that someone wasn't a girlfriend or her parents, it was her Uncle Mordecai. He was the one who saw her and spoke to her potential. When her girlfriends had no time for her, she could always turn to her Uncle.

She was a Jewish girl living it up in a Babylonian Palace. Do you think the young girls she came up with were cheering her on? I'm sure she had looks from the locals and dealt with jealously every day. She was living with all the other women competing to be Queen. All day, all the women around her, saw her as their competition. Her Jewish girlfriends thought she had sold out.

Maybe Esther pictured herself one day being married to a handsome Jewish man. Now, her whole life is centred around being groomed, to be married to a divorced, Babylonian King. She already knows her husband to be isn't the monogamous type.

Esther is eventually chosen as Queen and through a chain of events that her Uncle Mordecai coaches her through, she ends up saving her entire nation, including her jealous girlfriends and anyone else who spoke badly of her. Yes, she was pivotal in saving their lives too.

One of the reasons I love Esther's story so much is because I sometimes feel that running a fashion brand is not significant enough. It feels light compared to world-changing things I see others doing – you could say 'It's just clothes'. But I think of Esther who would have grown up thinking, 'It's just beauty. What can that do? Who can that save?' But look what God ended up doing with her beauty. Clothes and fashion have blessed so many people.

I've had women say they were excited about going into ministry and being ordained. They knew they had a call on their lives, but their biggest concern was what they would wear. I helped with that part. This journey is the reason I'm able to write this book!

It's not just beauty, clothes, fashion or whatever your creative thing happens to be. It is purpose! When you put it in God's hands, He can use it to change, save or impact a whole nation. For Esther, it was her literal nation. For me, it is the nation of Women in Ministry. Who is your nation? Who are your people that you will change, save or impact in a beautiful, powerful way?

God's Glory is in your story!

Before you were born
God had a dream.
The dream is you.
When God made you,
He wrapped a part of
His Glory inside of you and that's
what He sees when He sees you.

For this glory to be revealed, there are some things you have to go through. The table set out below should inspire you, whatever the stage of your life:

| The Person | The Glory | The Story |
Every time God sees:	*God sees:*	*What we see:*
Noah	Salvation	A just man who walked with God. Built an ark and *saved* his family and two of every kind of animal.
Joseph	Salvation	Shared his dreams that caused jealousy and envy in his brothers. He went from the pit to the palace and ended up *saving* his family from the famine.
Esther	Salvation	Selected and groomed in a harem of women, then chosen to be Queen. Used incredible courage, risked her life to *save* her people from annihilation.
Lazarus	Resurrection	A friend of Jesus who got sick and died. Jesus raised him from the dead so people would see and believe in the power of *resurrection*.

| Jesus | Salvation | Sent from Heaven, born of a virgin, endured many things, even the cross. He was crucified, died and rose again victorious. *Saving* the world from their sin and restoring our relationship and fellowship with God. *Jesus saved us!* |

It can be hard to see in the moment, but on reflection, we can see God's glory in these stories.

Think about what element of God's Glory is being revealed in your story and mine:

The Person Every time God sees:	The Glory God sees:	The Story What we see:
Camelle	Encourager	Desire for business from a young age. Started a fashion brand that developed into a Clergy Clothing Brand for Women. Writing, speaking, *encouraging* and inspiring other Christian creatives to Find their Divine Flow.
You		

Life is a wild, amazing adventure. Look at the clues and put the pieces of your puzzle together. Be on this journey with God so He can show you His beautiful plan. Seek His heart. Allow Him to get the glory out of your story.

Prayer
Lord, what do you see when you see me?
What is the glory in my story?
How will you use this to be a blessing in your Kingdom?

Chapter 6
Godfidence

The Simple Power of The Lord's Prayer

'After this manner therefore pray ye:
Our Father which art in heaven, Hallowed be thy name.
Thy kingdom come. Thy will be done in earth, as it is in
heaven. Give us this day our daily bread.
And forgive us our debts, as we forgive our debtors.
And lead us not into temptation, but deliver us from
evil: For thine is the kingdom, and the power, and the
glory, for ever. Amen.'
Matthew 6:9-13 KJV

I taught this simple prayer to my children when they were young, to give them a prayer to pray at bedtime, along with others. But Jesus didn't teach this prayer to children, He taught it to His disciples! I began to realise there is much more power in this prayer.

For a while now the part that says, "Give us this day

our daily BREAD" carried a deeper meaning for me. When I pray this prayer every day, the bread for me is symbolic of a number of things – Word, money, food.

Jesus also used this illustration:

'The Kingdom of Heaven is like the yeast a woman used in making bread. Even though she put only a little yeast in three measures of flour, it permeated every part of the dough.'
Matthew 13:33 NLT

Yeast = the fermenting agent used to raise dough.
Yeast = what Jesus compared the Kingdom of Heaven to.

Yeast is what turns the flour into bread. Without the yeast you have similar things but you don't have bread!

Even a little of the Kingdom of God (yeast) in your life (flour) makes all the difference. That's why this book is sprinkled with Kingdom principles. This is the most powerful ingredient needed in your life. It is the key to success, not just temporal success but also, and more importantly, eternal success.

Back to the Lord's Prayer - when we pray, "give us this day our daily bread", we are asking God to add some yeast to our flour and make it bread. Add some of the Kingdom of Heaven to our lives today. Tak what just looks like flour and raise it, bake it and make it bread. Bread that can be broken and shared to bless many.

Below are more examples of God taking nothing and making it something. Incredible!

Dust:

'And the Lord God formed man of the dust of the ground, and breathed into his nostrils the breath of life; and man became a living soul.'
Genesis 2:7 KJV

In the beginning God formed man from the dust (so similar to flour) of the earth. It wasn't even dirt, it was dust. You know when you clap your hands near flour and there's a cloud? God took the dust and formed man, then breathed into that dusty form and man became a living soul. A living soul that the Almighty God of Heaven communed with every day and they had a beautiful relationship.

Flour:

'So he went to Zarephath.
As he arrived at the gates of the village,
he saw a widow gathering sticks, and he asked her,
"Would you please bring me a little water in a cup?"
As she was going to get it, he called to her, "Bring me a
bite of bread, too."
But she said, "I swear by the LORD your God that I

single piece of bread in the house. And I
*ndful of **flour** left in the jar and a little*
ɔıı in the bottom of the jug. I was just
ɔ ..ıⅇering a few sticks to cook this last meal, and then
my son and I will die."
But Elijah said to her, "<u>Don't be afraid!</u>
Go ahead and <u>do just what you've said</u>,
but make a little bread for <u>me first</u>.
Then <u>use what's left</u> to prepare
a meal for yourself and your son.
For this is what the LORD, the God of Israel, says:
There will always be flour and olive oil left in your
containers until the time when the LORD sends rain
and the crops grow again!"
So she did as Elijah said, and she and Elijah and
her family continued to eat for many days.
There was always enough flour and olive oil left in the
containers, just as the LORD
had promised through Elijah.'
1 Kings 17:10-16 NLT

In this story lies the key to dealing with fear - it's
action. When she obeyed, she experienced a
lifesaving miracle for her and her son. In the face of
drought and death, they were sustained until the rain
returned.

Bread:

'And he commanded the multitude to sit down on the
*grass, and took the five **loaves**, and the two fishes, and*
looking up to heaven, he <u>blessed</u>, and <u>brake</u>, and <u>gave</u>

the loaves to his disciples, and the disciples to the multitude. And they did <u>all eat, and were filled</u>: and they took up of the fragments that remained twelve baskets full. And they that had eaten were about five thousand men, beside women and children.'
Matthew 14:19 KJV

It's time to Leaven Up! Yeast is sometimes referred to as 'leaven'. When you're leavened up you'll be baked and put through the fire of life but you'll come out as something God can use. He can bless you, break you and enable you to give your talents, your story and your gift to others so they can '*taste and see that the Lord is good*' (Psalm 34:8). They can eat and be filled.

Speak Life

Watch your words – '*out of the abundance of the heart the mouth speaks*'
Luke 6:45

I've grown up knowing that there is power in my words. I train my daughters to speak life. We don't say, "I can't" in our house. Instead we say, "I will try" or even more powerful, "I can do all things through Christ who strengthens me!" (Philippians 4:13).

God sees what we say

'Let the words of my mouth, and the meditation of my heart, be acceptable in thy sight, O Lord , my strength, and my redeemer.'
Psalm 19:14 KJV

This hit me so hard the other day. The words that come out of your mouth start from the things your heart meditates on. Your heart is the spiritual part of your mind. Your heart that pumps blood, can't meditate. Your mind meditates. Out of the abundance of the heart/mind your mouth speaks.

So, what this scripture is saying is, let what my mind meditates on, to the point that it captures my heart, let that form into the words that I speak. Let that be acceptable, not in God's hearing but in His sight. This tells me that when we speak, God sees what we say. Our words come out of our mouths and become things that God sees. Let what I say be acceptable in your sight Lord.

In the beginning, when God created the heaven and the earth, scripture records that God spoke, and then He saw what He spoke. We are created in His image, so what we speak also appears. Immediately that thing has life.

God breathed life into man and he became a living soul. We breathe that same God-breath every second and when words are mixed with that life-giving breath, we give life to words. God sees us creating every day.

So I ask you, what are you creating with your words all day long, creator? By the way, we have both life and death in the power of our tongue (Proverbs 18:21).

Let's speak life and create life everywhere we go, every time we open our mouths.

Daily Declarations

I read Terri Savelle Foy's book, 'Dream it. Pin it. Live it.' and learnt again about daily declarations and I wrote some powerful affirmations along with creating a vision board. One of these affirmations I spoke out loud for a few mornings was,

"House of ilona is the number one women's clergy brand in the world."

I did this declaration for two mornings. On the third morning I got a call from, and I quote "...the number one supplier of men's clergy shirts in the world". They wanted to launch into woman's clergy but after seeing what I was doing they wanted to partner with me instead.

What we declare out of our mouth, mixed with excitement, energy and faith is very powerful and we can literally watch it manifest in our lives.

If I'm completely honest with you... this experience scared me. After this I didn't do declarations for a while. I am someone who's not afraid of failure. I have enough tenacity, desire to learn and determination to pray through and make something work, or learn the lesson and move onto something better. What sometimes freaks me out is the magnitude of potential success.

It's not what if I fail but what if I succeed?

I've fallen flat on my face so many times that I now know how to get up - find one foot, lean my body weight on that knee to bring myself to the other foot and back up to standing. I'm well practiced in this. I know how to seek God when I'm flat on my face and have nowhere to look, but up to Him. I know how to extract powerful life changing lessons from my failures. What is more unfamiliar is the soaring posture. How do you seek God in the soar? When your path is lit, the bills are paid and you're living in your best life in the overflow, what does seeking look like from that perspective? I'm committed to learning how.

This is why I love to listen, learn from and study

successful Christian entrepreneurs of today and of the bible - Job, Abraham, Solomon, King David and Jesus. I know it can be more comfortable to think of Jesus as poor but you do realise when He was born He received gifts from kings; gifts of gold, frankincense and myrrh. I know the children's nativity is cute with three kings bringing three small gifts but these kings came bearing gifts on camels. PLURAL!

Jesus wasn't poor, Jesus was wealthy! When they had to pay taxes, Jesus said "give them the money". He had it!

'...he was rich...'
2 Corinthians 8:9 KJV

The gifts of gold, frankincense and myrrh were gifts FIT FOR A KING. Think about it.

"They entered the house and saw the child with his mother, Mary, and they bowed down and worshiped him. Then they opened their treasure chests and gave him gifts of gold, frankincense, and myrrh."
Matthew 2:11 NLT

My daily declarations in April 2019

Here I wanted to share my daily declarations. I change them every few weeks but tweak them nearly every day as I learn, grow and desire different things. So each day, I would say out loud:

- *Now I Am – (Rewiring my brain every day to align to my Divine Success)*
- *House of ilona is the number one women's clergy brand in the world.*
- *God, you are the Master Builder, build through me.*
- *You are the cornerstone of House of ilona.*
- *We are built on you, THE Solid Foundation; We will not be moved. We will not be shaken and We will not fail.*
- *House of ilona is the platform that will launch me.*
- *My life, my journey and my words are an inspiration to other Christian creatives, launching their dreams.*
- *Every day I commit at least fifteen minutes to writing three hundred words and speaking; in my journal, in my books, on platforms, through my podcast and one-to-one coaching.*
- *I have great expectations and live a designer life. I have things, things don't have me.*
- *I am grateful for everything we have. Thank you Lord.*
- *I am thoroughly enjoying my life!*
- *Everyday my relationships are growing better and stronger; my relationship with God, with myself, with Peter, with Mya and with Amelia-Rae. Plus family, friends, associates, those I coach and business relationships.*
- *Life is Good. Life is God.*

Can you begin to shape some daily declarations for yourself? What areas of your life do you want to see changed or improved? Speak Life to them every day. You have the breath of the Creator in you!

Dealing with doubts and Casting Cares

When you think there's not enough room,
that's a scarcity mentality.

There's no lack in God, only abundance.

I don't worry about copycats, I have trademarks and copyrights in place for that. I don't worry about people who have a similar vision, I encourage it; let's serve more people as we offer greater variety. If you provide the things I don't, I can refer people to your services. I don't believe in scarcity, I believe in abundance.

If no-one is doing a particular service or selling a particular product there are two reasons: firstly, you have found something no-one else has done and this could be an incredible opportunity. However, you need to be aware that if it is a brand new concept people need to learn about, there could be a period of drip feeding information to help people understand what it is, change behaviour and buy from you. Secondly, the reason could also be that people have tried it and it didn't work or there was no demand for it.

But if you've found something new that's needed, catch the wave and ride it.

What you have and how you deliver it is unique.
The difference between you and someone else is YOU.

Doubt

I posted the quote below on my social media to encourage someone else because it encouraged me:

Pay attention to the doubts, it's the enemy panicking about the giant leap of faith you're about to take!

As I was in this writing process of this book and nearing its completion, the doubts started to come in. First daily doubts, then hourly and almost every minute! "Does anyone need this? It's all been said before! Would anyone be interested in what YOU have to say? Why bother finish? Why not just keep it for your own records?"

God began to send confirmation. Every time I would get up from a writing session, the NEXT thing I heard was along the lines of what I had been writing. I knew (in my 'knower') that was God saying, "You're on the right track, keep going!!"

Then, then, then, I started to pay attention to the doubts... wait a minute! Every negative thought can be flipped and turned into a positive. Like Andrea says in her story (below) "...*It was as if she* (Camelle) *had been born with a gift of faith from birth. She would always be the one to see a glass half full and to believe for the impossible when everything looked bleak.*"

When I dwelt on doubtful thoughts they were heavy and negative, but when I flipped them around, as I illustrate below, they were massive and powerful:

Doubt thoughts	Faith thoughts
Does anyone need this anyway?	There are people who I don't know yet, who will read the words in this book and be encouraged to launch into their dreams and find their Divine Flow.
It's all been said before!	The principles have been said but my story hasn't been told yet!
Would anyone be interested in what YOU have to say anyway?	People are already interested and excited.

Doubt thoughts	Faith thoughts
Why bother finish?	It's not well started, it's well done! I will complete this assignment.
Why not just keep it for your own records?	I already have everything in my own records, this is for others to read. These are the chronicles of Camelle ilona Daley

What are the doubt thoughts in your head and what faith thoughts do you need to counteract them.

Doubt thoughts	Faith thoughts

Casting Care(s)

'Casting all your care upon him; for he careth for you.'
1 Peter 5:7 KJV

Growing up, I would always quote this scripture as "casting all your cares on Him". On closer study this actually says we should be casting, meaning this is a continual process. When there's something I'm concerned about it's easy to pray about it and give it to God one time, but then grab it back right away with worry. The Bible says "casting your care", singular not plural. Casting one care at a time.

'For my yoke is easy, and my burden is light.'
Matthew 11:30 KJV

We're conditioned to think things need to be hard and heavy but God said when we cast our burden on Him and take His yoke upon us, His yoke is easy and His burden is light. There are two things that I look for - "easy" and "light". When I'm doing something or approaching something new it should be easy and light. It can be light (as in the opposite of heavy), and when I have light (as in knowledge, information and training), this make the things much easier.

As a CEO I picture my problems being God's department and He's the expert in dealing with problems. I cast them His way, as in, I put them on the desk in His office and leave them there. When I feel He's taking too long, as in, I begin to worry, what I'm doing in effect, is, going into God's office, taking back the problem (I couldn't handle in the first place) and putting it back on my own desk, just so I have it to worry about. According to the scripture I have to keep "casting" and giving it back to Him.

When my business coach has a huge bill or problem

she says it like this; "God you have a problem!"

Initially, I thought, how rude to speak to God like this. She said it with such confidence, like it actually wasn't her problem at all; it really was His to deal with. As I grow in God, I fully understand how much He cares and wants to take care of us and supply all our needs, if we would only trust Him. Her level of confidence began to resonate with me.

Here's how it works for me:
- I have a problem, a situation, a bill, something that I cannot immediately handle myself, I need help!
- I choose to go to God (#DefaultSettings) for that help and I tell God about the situation. I pray, as in; I go to His office, lay every detail out on His desk with the supporting evidence and trust Him with it.
   - Side note: this could be what someone else has done to me or it could be totally and completely my fault, it doesn't matter to God, He specialises in all cases.
- I walk out, say Amen and TRUST that God can handle it, will handle it, is handling it and by faith has already handled it.
- The minute I start to worry and ponder and fret I have instantly taken back the problem, the detail and all the supporting evidence back onto my own desk, my plate and literally

on my shoulders. I have to keep casting it back to the new owner, God.

Prayer

(As the thoughts and worries <u>try</u> to bombard my mind)
Lord, I have trusted you with this situation. I am casting this thing I care about back to you because you care for me. This is no longer my problem it is yours and I trust you to handle it for me. I choose not to worry. I choose to trust you.
In Jesus name.
Amen

When the "casting" and the trust become your reality, God knows and He will handle your situation with excellence and precision. He will make all things work together for your good. Sometimes His answer and solution may not look favourable in the short term but God has His eye on your long game. In the coming days, months and even years, you'll be able to look back and know that 'the God solution' was the absolute best solution for you at that time, even if it didn't feel like it.

*****

Story Time

Have I always been this Godfident?
Andrea has known me since my early teens. Hear her perspective:

I've known Camelle since we were teenagers. Back then her nickname was 'faith baby'. It was as if she had been born with a gift of faith from birth. She would always be the one to see a glass half full, and to believe for the impossible when everything looked bleak.

I remember when she passed her driving test and needed a car. After much prayer she told me she believed God was going to give her a car but she should prepare for it. She went out and bought car mats and other bits and pieces for the car and had them sitting in the corner of her bedroom. I had never seen such dedicated belief before, and was eager to see the outcome. Not too long after that she called to say that unexpectedly a lady from her church offered to buy her a brand new car! That experience was one of the first times, as a young girl, I saw someone take real action on their faith. It's a story I remind myself of often when I'm hoping and believing for things. Sometimes God is giving us an instruction while we are waiting. Following that instruction builds our faith and puts us in a positive position to receive what He has for us.

Her faith has only grown over the years. For example, my husband and I are planning a career in music, which has its ups and downs. She came by one afternoon and we played her some of the music. Her energy and encouragement that day caused a huge shift in my perspective. Suddenly something I thought was a faraway dream became a much closer reality. Her genuine belief in us and the clarity in her vision of success was a game changer. She created a catalyst of faith and self-belief in the room that still continues to motivate me today. In a world that is sadly becoming increasingly self-centred, it's a rare thing to find someone who is truly excited about another person's dream.

More recently Camelle's friendship, faith, and inspiration have helped me navigate my way around being a new mum and wife. Her relentless faith is still there but now it is seasoned with the wisdom of running her own successful business, being a wife and mum of two! She's not afraid to challenge me when she hears fear in my voice, and she's not content until those fears are replaced by the 'power, love and sound mind' spoken about in 2 Timothy 1:7

Extract from my journal 12 Sept 2017

"Today I went to hang out with Camelle and my two goddaughters. But I got a lot more than I bargained for! Had a great day with the

girls, but it was the talk with Peter and Camelle that was so amazing. I saw two people passionate about their dreams and single-mindedly going after them. Turning off the noise of the crowd and 'Friends' and focusing hard on the path to their God given dreams.

They encouraged me to keep going, to keep writing, to not focus on always trying to be a better writer, but to be confident in who I am and my talent and everything I already have in my hands.

Camelle reminded me again, that God would not expose me to something that he wasn't ready to give me. She challenged me:
- *to not be afraid or feel overwhelmed,*
- *to not feel like my dream was far away in the distance and I would become a different person to achieve it.*
- *There was no need to be afraid of the future I was reaching for, I had to understand that I would still be me as I increase just with more success, wealth and accomplishments.*
- *She encouraged me to journal more.*

Camelle's hallmark for me is always making God her 'go to'. It seems like she instinctively reaches out to Him before anyone else. I believe this is what makes her words trustworthy, her love tangible, and her faith super-natural. A wise woman indeed.

Andrea Louise Francis, friend
Singer Songwriter
Instagram; @ms_andrealouise

I love watching Andrea grow in leaps and bounds and literally transforming as her mind-set shifts. Yes, I used to be called the "faith baby" and the "peace maker". I have always loved to believe God for things and situations and watch Him work. His word says, '.... prove me .....' (Malachi 3:10), I say "Okay then!"

Can you hear the themes from Andrea's story that we have already explored? I hope so, I hope this feels repetitive. Someone said that repetition is the mother of skill. One more time, repetition is the mother of all skill. Andrea talked about having faith in God in various areas, mind-set shifts, journaling and speaking life.

Upon reflection, the processes we go through in life are fantastic and so necessary. In the moment, the process can feel horrible and so hard. In order to make it easier, you need to adjust your mind-set while you are in the process, learn and grow through it.

Gold is refined in the fire, and I love gold. I love the product of the fire but the process of the fire, not so much. I love the change it produces but the pain it provides in the moment, not so much. When we see a child in a poverty-stricken country with nothing and they worship God with everything they have, we would say to them, "Wow you have nothing and you praise God like that – awesome!" They would turn to us in admiration and say, "Wow you have everything and you still praise God!" It's all a matter of perspective.

Believing when things are bad –
you have nothing but God.
Believing when things are good –
without God you would have nothing.

What does Godfidence look like?

- Having faith in God
- Continually "casting" each care
- Easy and light
- Understanding the purpose of the doubts
- Walking tall and confident knowing that God's got you!

Chapter 7
Be present

There is a question that changed everything and brought balance to my life:
How do you want your space to feel?

At a time in my life, my space felt blurry. There were no clear lines between home and work. I had moved my desk into the lounge for a photo shoot and a few weeks had passed, the desk was fast becoming a permanent feature. Definition was needed. As a young mum running my business from home, when I was working I felt guilty and when I was in mummy mode, I felt guilty for not working.

I had to rearrange my physical space. I moved my desk into a separate room in the house, this made work feel more like work and home feel more like home. I also set work hours. When it was time to pick up the girls from school and nursery (in those days) the business work stopped. I was in full on mummy mode.

I chose to be intentional and it worked, I was more present in each area of my life. I felt more fulfilled and less guilty.

Once I got an office outside our home, it was even easier to lock the door and go home.

- How does your creative/business/work space feel?
- How do you want it to feel?

Get this right and it has the potential to change everything for you.

We can't underestimate the power of creating the right environment to work and create in.

Go small then go home

It's the small, consistent, quiet, private, boring, routine and seemingly mundane actions that later heap huge success!!!

A common saying is, "go hard or go home". I say, "go small, then go home". I am a huge advocate of FOCUS. It's great setting goals and creating vision boards but it's not possible to focus on many things at once, not even our eyes can do that. You're more likely to hit something when you focus on it.

So, I choose to FOCUS. Focus on the one goal, out of the many - that one goal that will impact everything else when achieved.

Line up ten different objects in front of you and try focusing on all ten things at once - impossible! Focus on one thing and pour your energy into making that happen. You'll do it. You'll find your way around obstacles and when you tick that goal off, you can move on.

My top tips:
- Have priorities in life and know what's important to you
- Set goals that line up with your priorities, five to ten goals that you feel you could achieve in the next six to eighteen months
- Prioritize your goals to your top three and finally that ONE goal that if achieved would impact the rest
- Create a schedule based around your one goal and ensure you get balance across all areas of your life. Schedule your typical week, use colour codes for work, family, fun, church/ministry, couple time, me time and free time so you can see where your time is going and spot any imbalances
- Small things each day can make a massive impact. Thirty minutes of exercise each day doesn't sound like much but after a while this

> focused, consistent effort has a compounding effect
- *When you've done this you can – Go home.*

The "go hard or go home" gives the "going home" a negative connotation; as though, you're weak so go home. I say, "going home" means I've worked hard, now I deserve my rest. I have a balanced life, now I can go and be with my family, friends, and chill, read, sleep and not feel guilty.

Do these small, focused, consistent actions each day and then go home and chill.

Goals, Decisions, Focus and Routine

Focus on what you can control.
Trust God with the outcome.

Seed planting example:
- Decision - Find good ground or soil and get your best seed
- Focus - Plant your seed in that good ground
- Routine - Water it everyday

Trust God with the rest, He will bring the increase. We can't force a plant to grow, we do what we can and then we need to not just trust the process but also trust the God of the process. Trusting that:

- God will cause all things to work for our good
- God has a good plan with an expected end
- If we do our part God will do His part.

In business I have learnt there are things you can control and things you cannot control.

You can control;
- the quality of products and work you produce
- the quality and level of service you provide and
- the marketing you put out to give your business exposure.

You cannot control:
- who buys from you and
- when they buy from you.

Depending on how you view goals, a goal can feel like it may or may not happen. It has to fit the SMART criteria of being **s**pecific, **m**easurable, **a**chievable, **r**ealistic and **t**imed. But when I make a decision, such as, "I'm going to write a book this month", some would argue, that's a goal! Maybe, but I just prefer to use the word decision. It's a fixed action not a moveable goal. I don't set many goals; I have one to two every twelve weeks.

I really love working to a twelve-week plan as so much can be achieved in that period. You can write a book or transform your body. I read the book *12*

Week Year by Moran and Lennington, it made a big impact on me. I love to plan and schedule, but what I learnt from reading this book helped me break things down in a great way and made me even more productive.

Having a purpose statement for my life is great, it helps me to bring everything into alignment. Having one focus for twelve weeks is powerful. You have something to concentrate on each day and you'll have something tangible in the end.

Routine

Getting into a routine is hard at first, until you find your rhythm; then it becomes second nature. However, once the routine is broken, then you need to find your flow again.

The Presence of this present day

The children of Israel had to collect enough manna each morning, sufficient for that day alone (Exodus 16). Jesus prayed along the same lines, "*Give us this day our daily bread*" (Matthew 6:11). Jesus also said to seek first His Kingdom, righteous living, and everything you need will be added (Matthew 6:33). He also taught us not to worry about tomorrow, focus on today (Matthew 6:34).

There is such incredible power in this very moment. We need to understand the power today holds. Stop living in yesterday and tomorrow.

As a businessperson this is a hard concept to grasp. We are so focused on what's next, future planning, short, mid and long term goals that we barely see what's in front of us because we're so focused on the next customer, the next quarter or acquiring the next contract.

Focus on now

A few years ago, someone recommended to me the book *Jesus Calling*. I was going on holiday and purchased the audiobook version, not realising it was a daily journal. This book was filled with powerful daily words of inspiration from God, to shift your thinking for that particular day. I could not put it down. It was power tips on steroids. It was intense to say the least.

Two of the 'months' that I listened to in this audiobook, back to back, focused on living in the now and being present. I could literally feel my mind-set shifting!

I was so used to planning and being a couple steps, weeks, month and years ahead of the game. These words and scriptures bombarding my mind through this audiobook devotional were now telling me to focus only on today. This was a totally new way of thinking. A new way of doing business, even. Focus on today and trust God with the past and future.

The past

Forget the things which are behind. Stand where you are and press forward:
- We can learn from the past but we can't change it.
- If we messed up, we manage the consequences intentionally.

The future

There is so much we cannot control:
- Our present actions are creating our future.
- What you will be, is being created in the patterns of today.

Making plans

I can make blue-sky predictions all day long but they don't mean much. There are so many moving parts to business, micro and macro factors within and outside of our control. When making plans, it's more powerful to do it from today's perspective.

For example:

How much will your business make in five years?

Blue-sky says;
£5,000,000

Projecting from today's perspective says;
For the past three years Company XYZ has doubled their income.
2016 - £20,000
2017 - £40,000
2018 - £80,000
So using this information, in five years at steady growth they should hit at least
£2,560,000

Leaning in from historical information and today's perspective is a much more powerful way to predict future projections rather than plucking figures out of the air.

Press from the position of today

When you press from today into the future it's a more realistic and measured way to view and plan for the future. Look for patterns and plan ahead. Don't spend too much time planning. Make your plans and leave room for God to edit.

Don't worry about tomorrow. All you have is the present, focus on being all you can be in this moment.

Not your typical business teaching - rather, this is more like biblical business teaching. When I try and plan the future it's a struggle. Who knows what will happen politically, economically, socially? What will the trends be in two to five years? When I live in this day and this moment and do all I can NOW, I experience incredible results and so much peace.

I do have a business plan and strategy for the future, when I'm focused on that plan it feels like such a struggle. There is so much that's out of my hands. I sell clothing; I don't know who will purchase from me today or this week. I do all I can do in terms of marketing etc., but there are still no guarantees. Business is a risk and takes so much faith.

I like to focus on doing the best I can today. Today is what I have. That's in my hands, that's what I can control.

The bigger picture is important. It sets your intention and your 'Why'. It's your destination. You can check that your GPS for the day is pointing in the right direction and then you get your head down and focus on the road and manoeuvres in front of you.

Great quotes I've heard along my journey:
'Bit by bit it's a synch'
'Slow and steady wins the race'
'Enjoy – don't endure – the journey'.

How do you want your space to feel?
What's your one goal/decision for this week?
What's your one goal/decision for the next 12 weeks?
What CAN you do that is within your control?
What do you want to happen that is outside of your
control? (It's good to identify the difference)

Chapter 8
Finding Fulfilment

It is so important to do what you love and love what you do. The life of an entrepreneur isn't for everyone but whatever your passion or profession, do it with all your heart and as unto the Lord.

I've wanted to write a book for years, share the various keys I've gleaned along my journey. I went on a Coaching Retreat with The Business Bishop, Bishop Wayne Malcolm, came home and wrote the majority of this book in about three weeks. It was just flowing out of me. But, during this time it felt like everything else in my life was on hold. I was being invited to more speaking engagements, which helped my book writing process and helped to define my message. After that intense three weeks I got busy with life again. Weeks were passing and I hadn't done much more writing. I was starting to feel stuck. Will I ever finish the book?

I then had the idea to ask my Facebook friends, "If I were to write a book on my entrepreneurial journey what would you like to read about?" The flood of comments that came in helped me complete my manuscript. To be honest, I had no idea some of those people answering would have any interest in a book written by me. Also, most of the themes had already been covered in my manuscript so far, so I knew I was on the right track, so I thought it would be a good idea to use this chapter to answer some of those questions.

BUSINESS

How did the idea come to you and evolve?

I have always had a love for fashion, clothing and style. I would be sitting in conferences, listening to preachers and by the side of my notes designing what I think the preacher could be wearing. This has always been in me. When I studied my roots, I learnt that my paternal grandfather was a renowned tailor in Jamaica and my maternal grandfather was a preacher. It's just IN ME!

When my friend Chantel was ordained as a Youth Minister and needed to wear a collar once a month, she came to me and said, "I don't want to wear the ugly shirt, please design me something!" I made her a simple black, knee length dress with a white collar. After the service she reported that everyone was going crazy for this dress!! I was shocked, it's one of the simplest things I had made. To see if anyone else would be interested, I put it on my website as something I would make-to-order and deliver in two to three weeks. I then ran some Facebook Ads (a skill that I was learning at the time), targeting women in ministry in the UK, USA, Canada and Australia. Within a week I had so many orders I had to shut the Ads down because I couldn't sew fast enough!

Once I knew there was a demand, I invested in manufacturing and production. I built a list of targeted people who I could continue to market to, and I kept listening to their needs and following the changes in demand.

I found people who wanted what I had, connected, stayed connected and kept plugging in. I remember a point in the early days when I nearly quit, but I kept going. A year to the day later, all kinds of people started to show up saying, "I've been watching you for a year!" Just think - what if I'd quit and given-up? I was so happy I didn't quit, now I was seeing the fruit of my labour.

Who inspired you?

I am truly inspired by anyone doing what they love to do and what they were born to do. I get this from my Dad, he would be mesmerised by comedians who got paid to laugh and make people laugh.

I was inspired at seven years old, sitting with my Mum on a red, London, double-decker number 264 bus. A lady walked on, in a sharp suit and an elegant bag for her paperwork. My little self said, "That's what I want to be when I'm older!" Didn't know what she did but she had a commanding presence and just looked like she knew who she was, where she was going and what she was doing. She looked like a boss!

I am inspired by God, the bible and prayer. For years I thought I was strange (or slightly obsessed with business) because I'd sit and listen to a preacher, preaching the Word of God and all I could hear was business principles. I could hear how this Word could be related to a new way of doing things or I could hear an answer to a problem and when I applied it to my work, it worked!

I am also inspired by my potential and the potential I see in others.

Where do your ideas come from?

My ideas come from what's selling and what my clients are asking for. I listen to and respond to the demand and I grow organically by continually doing this. I started House of ilona with one design that sold really well. Then I tweaked it slightly from the feedback I received. Again it sold really well. Next, my clients were asking for the shape of one dress but the length of another: the 'Clergy Tea Dress' was launched. The dresses arrived in the middle of the summer, I launched them on the Friday afternoon, left to spend time with family for the weekend and when I got back they were sold out! I followed the demand and it worked.

How did you know your idea would succeed?

I didn't know it would succeed. I hoped and believed it would - I tried lots of things. I would quit things that weren't working but I <u>never quit my hunt for purpose and fulfilment.</u>

Business is a risk. Producing bulk quantities of stock is a risk. I don't know who will buy or if anyone will buy. Just because people bought before doesn't mean they'll buy again. I calculate my risk, backed with research and prayer and I make moves.

I didn't move the business out of my house until:
- I absolutely had to, due to capacity and
- I could easily afford it.

I didn't make the move of my stock out the office to a warehouse until:
- I absolutely had to, due to capacity and
- I could easily afford it.

What do you do when you're frustrated with the pace of progress?

I remember this quote often, "slow and steady wins the race". When I was younger I was always in a rush, just in a rush to get to places and in a rush to get to places in life, where I felt I should be.

I process the process and it helps me to understand what's going on. I'm also learning how to be more present. Being present is such a big theme in my life and in my blogs. Being present in this present moment, because this moment is a gift! So rather than rushing ahead and being in such a rush all the time (I feel like I have been in a rush all my life), I'm learning to slow down and appreciate where I am and trust that God is working all things out for my good.

Even in this present moment of writing and reflecting, God has me here for a reason and I need to observe, absorb, receive and learn all that I can from this moment. Then, when my season is complete, I am released to move on to the next moment and receive the new lessons life needs to teach me. If I didn't learn, I'd have to do re-takes – I may not be in a rush in life but I'm also not trying to delay my own progress.

I do my best to grasp this moment, live in this moment, see the tree swaying outside my window, see the sky and be in this moment of this day. Understand and embrace this moment, this day and this time and what it's all about. Tomorrow isn't promised to me, today is. Today is my present from God, it's my gift. Rather than pining for the next gift (tomorrow), let me unwrap, learn, study and enjoy this gift of today.

I know that "my time" will come, I know it. I feel guaranteed by God that everything I want will happen. It's not a matter of 'if', it's a matter of 'when'. So because I trust Him with my time and I believe my times are in His hands, I've seen Him do so many things in my life, I just know God is in control, taking care of me. He's in the detail of the details of my life. So I don't have anything to worry about. I'm moving at His pace and I trust Him with what I'm hoping for. I embrace this moment and I drain everything I can out of this moment, live it to the full and keep going. The process seems slow but when I look back I can truly see how far I've come.

Study the pace of your own progress in light of your journey, not in light of someone else's. I remember speaking to a friend, she said, "I'm thirty-five and not married yet with any children!" That statement was in the light of certain friends around her of the same age. In that light, her life looked empty. But when I reviewed her thirty-five years in the context of her own dreams and purpose and highlighted certain facts such as, the mission trips she had been on, all that she's been able to study and accomplish through her writing and range of jobs, in that light, her life had been full and fulfilling. So it all depends on how you are viewing your progress.

I am like the character, Joy, from the movie, "Inside Out". I love how she sees life, she can put a positive spin on absolutely anything. I love this and I've always been like this. When my friends want a sad moment and want to stay there, they don't come to me. When they're looking for some light in the midst of darkness, I'm their girl!

What is the source of your success?

This is the essence of this book. There's no secret here. IT'S ALL GOD!! I give Him all the glory. Yes, I do the work, but God gives me the increase in so many ways; direction, inspiration, encouragement when I'm down along with the unseen work and connections I cannot explain. Every day I work hard to REMEMBER that it is God who "gives me the power to get wealth" (Deuteronomy 8:18)!

Can you share the importance of the mundane?

There is a lot of repetition in business. The creative side and the client interaction provide variety, but I have to choose to be in it for the long haul.
For me, that means: analysing your numbers each week, keeping an eye on stock and doing stocktakes,

monitoring suppliers and making sure we're getting the best deals, answering repetitive emails, getting catalogue requests out and other repetitive jobs.

If repetition is the mother of skill then the opposite must be true; inconsistency is the father of incompetence.

I cannot count the amount of times I see people and they ask, "Are you still doing the fashion line?" It seems more acceptable to quit than stay at something for years. There is power in consistency! I am known for what I do. It can be mundane but as a creative person I find ways to make it more exciting.

I remember reading about this in a book and praying, "God I want to make money while I sleep", and I remember the first time waking up to orders people placed overnight (while I slept). I was so grateful to God. I prayed it and it was actually happening. Another book outlined the concept of working one time and getting paid over and over again. So I prayed that too. Many years later, I still get paid for designs I sketched years ago.

There was an issue though. People loved these designs so much that they asked for more of the same - the same dress in navy blue, in white and I wasn't getting to be creative. My design muscle wasn't being flexed because I was just reproducing the same style in different colours. So, again, I prayed: "God thank you so much for what I have, but I'm creative and I'm getting bored. You made me creative and I want to use my creativity in my work."

Then someone asked about House of ilona making capes. I knew the long type wasn't our style, but I had already made some non-clergy capes in the past. I took an image of one of my old capes, put it in Photoshop, changed the colour from orange to black. I then added a white square for the clergy collar and put it on Facebook... I nearly crashed my website because people were searching for it on our website and complaining they couldn't find the cape!! "Where is it?" "How much is it?" "How quickly can you get one to me?"

People loved the idea so we went into production. We did black, navy blue and black and white dogtooth. People loved the concept of having a clergy cape and began to share great uses for it, which helped me in my marketing. They said they could use them for funerals when they were at the graveside, for outdoor Christmas Carol services and generally out and about in the community.

Everything felt new again, I was designing and producing; I had new images and new marketing. It was a breath of fresh air, and cut through the mundane.

Consistency is boring but can pay really well.

People often forget that excellence is a result of grafting, repetition and recording. Do you believe the final flourish the world sees is as important as the hours of practicing and perfecting?

The book, *Outliers,* by Malcolm Gladwell talks about the ten thousand hours that you put in to become an expert. I remember a year or so ago getting to the point where I felt like I had put in my ten thousand hours and transitioned to a new place in business. I felt like I had become an expert in my field - it was a good feeling. This is how much of me that I had invested into women's clergy wear. Learning it, selling it, designing it, producing it, marketing it and being in contact with women of God in ministry.

It was a landmark. It is many, many, thousands of hours of practicing and perfecting and yes, the world sees the final flourish, but there are a lot of hours that go into it. It's important to look at the amount of hours that you have already spent in your life in certain areas and certain things, because you are probably an expert or almost an expert, a skilled craftsperson in a certain field, one of the top people, because of the amount of hours you put in.

My Aunt has been a legal secretary for thirty years and that's way more than ten thousand hours in that field. She is a master at that, but she is also a phenomenal coach. In my teens and early twenties I was subject to her coaching. She was constantly disrupting my world with her questions about the jobs I was doing, such as, "Is this really what you want to do? Can you see yourself doing this for the next ten to twenty years? Are you satisfied?" Her questions kept pushing me to find work I loved. Thank you Auntie!

I believe that those two elements of her life - legal secretary and coaching, in the not too distant future, will come together in a beautiful way, whereby she could even coach some of the legal secretaries who were becoming displaced due to job cuts and workplaces downsizing. But with her joy, energy and experience in the field, I believe she will be able to help a lot of people when her coaching skills and many years of experience come together.

We should never underestimate the power of the hours we have put into various things in our life.

It is possible to feel that what you are doing is so mundane, for example, "I've just been a teacher for the last twenty years" or "I've been a technician for thirty-five years." It can feel so mundane, but there is something God can do with all that skill, time and energy. God can take that and use it for His Glory in a way that makes you very happy and fulfilled.

What worked and what didn't work?

What worked is listening to my customers. What sometimes didn't work is listening to customers!

I have learnt to listen to the majority of customers. When a lot of people ask for a specific item and I mass-produce it, that works. When one person asks for something specific, that is great for one and two, but doesn't necessarily result in mass-market appeal.

What has also served me well in business is being a continual learner. I have tried and tested so many things and have chosen to learn from the various things that did and didn't work. It has made me a better entrepreneur and a better person.

How do you stay motivated?

I am naturally an upbeat, motivated person, if I'm down, it's written all over my face and it's really hard to hide! I'm generally motivated and I love motivating other people. When I feel down, all it takes is for me to see someone else in a bad situation and I can't help but to encourage him or her. Then the same encouragement that's flying out of my mouth to them, I hear it too and end up encouraged. I am very much about motivating, inspiring and encouraging, to my core, so I work hard to keep myself motivated, inspired and encouraged. I work on:

- Pursuing my purpose
- Staying focused on what I'm doing and my mission
- Being prayerful
- Having a mission that I'm working toward and
- Listening to business training, preaching and anything that keeps me up is a massive help.

When motivation runs out, discipline must kick in!

FINANCES

How do you keep on top of finances?

I've had to force myself to monitor my outgoings ferociously, which I do a few times a week. I meet with my Fashion Business Consultant, David Jones, once or twice a month and he will grill me on the numbers. I have to come to that meeting prepared and I need to be able to answer his questions. He always wants to see the numbers. "The business talks to you, listen" he says often.

There are some incredibly smart business people out there who can read a business just by the numbers

(I'm working on becoming one of these people). I had the opportunity to speak to an equity advisor after he conducted a workshop I attended. I showed him my catalogue and he loved the business right away, he was actually in ministry for ten years. He asked what my turnover was, when I told him he raised his eyebrows, and then he went in. (As the Bible says about the woman at the well in John 4:29, "he told me all I ever did" - lol). He told me:

- how much profit I was making,
- how many staff I had and
- what I needed to do - release cash, triple the business and take it to ten million.

It was such a simple strategy too, he said, "It's doable. I see hundreds of businesses and it's rare that I come across something I've not seen before, something I wish I'd thought of." This was a huge compliment.

How do you count the cost of doing business?

'For which of you, intending to build a tower, sitteth
not down first, and counteth the cost,
whether he have sufficient to finish it?
Lest haply, after he hath laid the foundation,
and is not able to finish it, all that behold it begin to
mock him, Saying, This man began
to build, and was not able to finish.'
Luke 14:28-30

Before you begin any venture, it's important to do your research, do your due diligence and, as the bible says, "count the cost"; the cost in terms of time, money and energy. Research and count as much as possible, know as much as you can, and know what you don't know – the gaps and unanswered questions. Do a SWOT Analysis and know what is outside of your control. The SWOT looks at internal Strengths and Weaknesses, as well as external Opportunities and Threats. We don't know what the future holds, but it's important to count the cost as much as possible at the beginning.

The bible says people will mock and laugh at you if you don't count the cost first. Know what's needed, not just to get started, but also to finish. Keep monitoring as you go, to see what else you need along the way.

What resources did you use to build financially?

This was always a challenge, as I've cash-flowed the business. What comes in is what is used to produce more. We've had two to three small loans, but mainly cash-flowed. That's why it has seemed (to me) like we've grown so slowly. But I always encourage myself that "slow and steady wins the race." Please note, I don't enjoy slow! But this speed has me paying attention, learning as I grow in business and grow in God.

BALANCE

How do you find balance?

Balance is really important to me. I find my balance in prayer; I find my centre in prayer, when I can just pour it all out.

Lists are also a great tool for me. I always recommend to friends, when they are feeling overwhelmed and unbalanced, to make a list. Prioritise the list and get to work. If anything else comes to mind that's not included, don't fret, just add it and re-prioritise the list.

A good list is a way to release what's going on in your head when thoughts are messy, scrambled and everything feels urgent. Take a brain dump and get every bit of it out into a long list. When you can't think of anything else, the list is done. I like to prioritise 1-5, as in the example below:

1 = do it now, as soon as I've done prioritising this list do this/these actions

2 = do it next, by the end of the day

3 = do these tomorrow

4 = do these the next day

5 = do these next week or outsource or don't bother.

Next, I re-write the list in order of priority with a square box before each item so I can tick off as I go along and I keep myself accountable.

I like the list because it's all written down so nothing will be missed. Those thoughts are now in order of priority, so I don't need to worry and stress about them anymore. If someone asks me about something, I can say, "It's on my list to do tomorrow," and I sound in control without the internal panic.

How do you balance family and work?

As I mentioned in Chapter 7, there was a time when I felt completely unbalanced. When I was home and in "mummy mode" I felt like I wasn't doing enough for the business. Then when I was working in the business I felt like I wasn't doing enough with the children. I just felt guilty all the time! I had to reorganise my space and time. I had to choose to be all in when it was work time and choose to be all in when it was mummy time. It took time and discipline, but worked and I felt so much more balanced.

I also keep balance by doing regular check-ins, by asking and checking: how's my marriage, my relationship with my children, family, friends, with my God and with myself? Where's my personal care time? One of the ways I do this is by scheduling my average week on one sheet of paper and colour coding it. This shows me where most of my time is going and areas that are lacking and non-existent.

Try it on some paper or in an Excel spread sheet (I do love an Excel spread sheet). Along the top fill out: Sunday to Saturday, while down the left side, fill out 5am to 10pm (or whatever times work for your life). Then fill in what an average week currently looks like for you. For me, this changed drastically when my children were babies, compared to now that they're in school full-time.

Colour code:
- God time
- Me time
- Couple time
- Family time
- Social time
- Work time
- Gym time
- Reading/hobby time and
- Sleep.

It should be filled in and be very colourful. If you work full-time, a lot will be work time, but it's good to see what you're doing with the rest of your time on an average week. Visually you can see how balanced you are.

What is your support system?

Physically, we live in different cities from our families. My extended family is seventy miles south and Peter's extended family is seventy miles to the north (we like to say we "met in the middle"). So we don't have family close by, but we have different types of support systems in place. Physically, we have church friends and friends who have become like family to us, who help us with the children when we want a night out or our work commitments clash.

From a distance, I lean on my sisters for emotional support. Even though they're not close by, I know I can pick up the phone and call them. I may not call them all the time, but I know they're there; I can call or send a WhatsApp voice note. These conversations and swapping notes on life help me know I'm not alone. Calls to aunties, uncles, cousins, family WhatsApp groups and social media really help me stay connected. When we meet up it's like no time has passed because we've stayed connected.

My business also has support systems and teams, most of which aren't close physically. My Fulfilment warehouse is in the next town, my website tech support is in LA on the other side of the world, as are my manufacturers. This is my business support system. My manufacturers are the ones who bring my ideas and designs to life on a mass scale and keep my production going and flowing. I have people who help with different areas of the business. I have one sister who helps with photography, another with graphic design via their own businesses.

The different time zones work to my advantage. For example, we have a huge percentage of our clients based in the USA, so peak times for web activity can be in the night/morning for me which is evening/night in the USA. So having web support State side works well because peak time surges is where we can have issues and the US team is working then. If it was a UK based team we'd have to wait until morning and may not be as responsive at these peak times.

My Fashion management consultant, David Jones has been an incredible support. In the early days of business I'd speak about my business issues to anyone who would listen, because I needed an outlet. I'd get back anything from blank faces to bad advice. So having a professional advisor to meet with once or twice a month and available on the phone at any time, was a game changer (and means I can speak to my friend and family about things other than my business issues!)

God is my internal support system, all ... day ... long. I'm constantly checking in and acknowledging Him, no matter who I'm speaking to; I'm listening and making sure I'm staying in the Divine Flow.

How do you balance staying focused on the vision, discipline and time management?

Most of the time it's not hard to stay focused on the

vision - I engage my focus. Most of time it's right there. It's women in ministry, serve them and provide clothes for them. Our mission statement is: *helping women look good on the outside is our business, helping women feel good on the inside is our heart.*

I reconnect with the vision and mission before each meeting. If I feel like I'm going off track I check back in with the vision.

BUT... I am a very creative person. I am multi-skilled and multi-talented and I have lots of creative ideas. So staying focused has been a challenge, because a new shiny idea can come to me or be presented to me and it's exciting! Thoughts of how I could make this work with what I'm doing now are tempting but my experience now forces me to stay focused. Anything new which does not complement my vision causes a division.

I have been distracted before. Now I practice looking further down the road - checking in with my own personal life goals and making sure things line up with that.

In the early days, an easy place for me to get distracted was with marketing opportunities. As a business, you get targeted with many opportunities from advertisers. Now, my first question is, "What percentage of your readers or listeners are women in ministry?" This is my target market and allows me to be highly selective and targeted when it comes to my advertising focus.

When it comes to my life goals or decisions, I can say "for this year, it's about focusing on my business and helping other creatives launch their businesses and dreams". This is the reason I'm writing this book this year and doing business coaching because that's in line with my goals.

Recently, a company approached me to sell another product range. They said, "You'd be great because you already sell. Read up on this and do this training, commit a couple of hours etc." It sounded great. But after a conversation with my accountability partner, suddenly this "opportunity" felt more like a distraction from the goals and decisions I had set. The key here for me was not making a decision in the moment, but stepping away, out of the environment, to see things clearer.

So, to stay disciplined I remain accountable to:
- my work hours - so when it's work time I WORK
- the office space - being in my office, which I have to pay for each month. This also helps me to be disciplined. Once the children have been taken to school and I go into my office, I go into work mode
- producing the product and marketing – I can't control what people buy and how much they

spend (that was a revelation). I am responsible for the energy and the effort that I put in. I produce the product and do the marketing but I can't control who buys what. But I believe if I stay consistent with what works and pay attention to changes, my hard work will pay off.

It was harder to keep the discipline when the children were younger and I was at home, but it was still possible. I had to give myself grace and flexibility. When children are young, things change - they can get sick and have off days. For example, I could have a good plan and schedule that would work for a few weeks, and I'm in the flow. Suddenly a child could get chicken pox or catch a bug. I would just have to write off a week or two. I may be able to send out an email here or there, but if my children need me they are my priority.

Try to stick to your schedule, but be flexible, because life happens. Don't beat yourself up because you didn't get through your to-do list. Have lots of grace.

What are the challenges you faced with having young children?

When my girls were at nursery I had three hours, minus pick up and drop off times, so it was really two hours and forty minutes. I did the things I couldn't do with the little ones around, like an hour at the gym (my me-time) and I could return phone calls and do the things that needed quiet concentration time.

I had to plan what I could do when the children were around, such as things I could do while they were sleeping. In those early years I needed more patience than drive! Because THINGS CHANGE and they change so much and so fast, before you know it, three months have passed, then a year has passed.

In those very early days with a new-born, some mums seem like super mums; they've got everything together, all the time, including themselves. Then there are other mums (now my hand is raised) who just didn't feel like they'd accomplished anything, other than waking up, then getting dressed (sometimes) - just making it through to the end of the day was an accomplishment.

Even now, at the time of writing this, my girls are six and nine years old. They go to school from 8:40am to 3:10pm and I work in between. I can have a great work flow and schedule lined up, then one gets sick and is off for a week, the other one catches it, (not at the same time obviously, lol that would be way too organised). So then, it's another week off and that's usually followed by the school holidays (it's happened, more than once).

Life comes in seasons and stages. You can't compare yourself to somebody in a whole different phase of life, for example, with grown up children or to a single person.

Be flexible! Be kind to yourself!

HARD TIMES

What motivated you to keep going when things were difficult?

God and His Word are a huge motivation to me.

Our clients keep me going with their kind words, emails, encouragement and prayers.

Lack of other options keep me going. What else would I do? I love ministry, fashion, marketing and business. I get to do all those things in this business every day. If I shut up shop, what else would I do? What about the women who have been following us for years and don't know that one day they will be ordained? What if the day they need me I'm not there, because I got discouraged, because I got "weary in well doing" (Galatians 6:9)! I won't stop until God says it's time.

Have you ever reached breaking point, what did it feel like, how did you make it through?

There are three major times that I feel like I came to the breaking point and really questioned if I should still be doing this. The point came where I prayed the prayer:

"Lord, is this what I should still be doing? Do I stop? Do I continue? Please confirm because it's hard. This feels like a natural place to shut down before I take on another wave of production".

The breaking point is not fun but it stretches you. When you hit that ceiling in business or in life and you're not sure whether to continue or stop, you are at a crossroads and the next decision you make is crucial. If you can break through that breaking point, you will reach the point of no return. You will have overcome this whole level (like in a video game) and you've cleared it. This point will be marked. It's a milestone - you never have to go back further (unless you choose to), you have cleared this level.

I've learnt to hold things with an open hand. I don't want to hold something so tight that I can't hear God say, "Release". It could be the natural end to a thing, the end of a season, or it could be the ceiling that is the floor of the next level.

What principles do you use for establishment of your success?

Focus is a huge key for me. I've been focused on my House of ilona Clergy brand niche for the last ten years. Now things are working well, and, to an extent, flowing without me. So it's giving me space and time to share from my experience and pour into others, write this book and coach entrepreneurs. But getting to this place took ten years of focus. As I stretch into this new area I will still be focused on helping Christian creatives launch dreams. It ties in beautifully to the themes of the last ten years.

Balance is needed across all areas of life. One area of my life can't be in competition with another. The pursuit of finding balance is a worthwhile one. What balance looks like for me may not be what balance looks like for you. For me, it has changed over the last five years from when I had a new-born, and in the next five years I'll have a teen and pre-teen.

Balance don't juggle!

Consistency is another huge key for me; being consistent on social media, in production quality and service level. Making it better but consistent, so people know what they're getting. Being consistent also means that my company is the go-to recommended company for what I do.

What are the pitfalls and how to overcome them?

There are various pitfalls; pitfalls people know about, some you can read about. You need training and education from people who have gone before you, in your field, similar fields and totally unrelated fields. There are signposted pitfalls in the road ahead of you, but if you don't know what you're looking for and how to navigate them, it's easy to fall.

To avoid pitfalls stay educated, stay on the pulse of your industry; know what's going on. Reading will help you understand the pits others have fallen into, why they fell and how they got out.

Then there are pitfalls people place in front of you intentionally and unintentionally. A pitfall is not a permanent situation and doesn't determine the end of a thing, your business or dream. With the right information you can navigate your way around and or out of it.

I'm such an optimistic person that I believe there's a way out of any pitfall. My God brain says, "There is a way that all these things can work out for the good!"

The answer is in the question, how do you overcome a pitfall? You do just that, you overcome it. You overcome through prayer, fasting, seeking wise counsel, getting advice, help and guidance through people, books and research. Do whatever you physically, spiritually, mentally can, to get out of the pit you have fallen into. Remember it's temporary.

What failures have you encountered?

I've messed up on marketing; there are things that I agreed to that I shouldn't have and it ended up costing me so much money. At one stage, we were completely off balance as a business, doing more marketing than we had products.

Marketing and the production need to work together. There have been times when I've had more product than marketing and times that I've had more marketing than product; neither is nice! At one point I had so much publicity and not enough products to fulfil the demand, but I made lemonade from these lemons and built a huge waiting list. This meant that when the products came back in stock we could sell right away.

Another time, we had a major communication issue with a new manufacturer. They had over manufactured! I wanted a wide range of sizes - from 4 to 32 in certain clergy blouses in standard colours like black, white and navy blue. Then, in the brighter colours I wanted to have a narrower range of sizes like 12 to 24. This would have been a perfect plan, but instead, they reproduced every size in every colour, which was double the amount of manufacturing and cost. But they had done it and this bill needed to be cleared before more work could be done.

I learnt (the hard way) the level of detail I needed to go into with this manufacturer. Most manufacturers do this automatically when there's left over fabric, they just keep making. We now have an agreement that they check with me first, before overproducing.

How do you manage the highs and lows?

There can be high highs and low lows, but generally everything is pretty even keeled. The high highs can be great sales, great publicity or an amazing testimonial, photo or video. That's just such a high for me. I remember a picture of a lady minister in Hawaii with her bright pink House of ilona 'Clergy Tea Dress', surrounded by about thirty young girls in white dresses, standing on a beach. Fifteen girls on either side of her and it was just an amazing picture. There was also another picture of a client wearing our 'Pink Clergy Tea Dress' whilst receiving her MBE from Prince William. This incredible picture is on the wall in my office and really sums up the word I first received about the business ten years ago, "House of ilona, House of beauty for earthly and spiritual royalty."

The lows can happen if something goes wrong, I process the process and stretch myself to find the lesson. I speak to people who can naturally hear the lesson because I want to learn from what I did wrong. I want to learn so that I don't do it again, so I can tell someone else, "Look, there's a pitfall in the road just there!" "There's an obstacle that is going to be placed right in front of you, as you turn left, slow down because you're going to find an obstacle and what you need to do is this, that and the other."

Make the most out of the low, until the low turns into a high!

What did you do when you felt like quitting?

I go back to the reason I started in the first place. I've not yet completed my assignment so I know I need to keep going. Sometimes a word, a song or a good motivational push gets me going again. But at other times when I've felt like quitting, I gave myself time. Time to dig in a little deeper. What's really going on here? I'll journal and pray it through. I start asking myself that 'why' question. Why am I feeling like this? Why has this happened? One of two things will happen; 1) I'll receive answers or 2) I'll receive peace about the situation because I've taken the time to understand. I may not have the answer but the peace really helps with the waiting.

SOCIAL MEDIA

Where do you start with a social media strategy and what to post?

Be known for something. Be the lady who... and the guy who...

In the early days of Facebook I would share on my personal profile all the time about my work and the things connected to it. I'd share fabrics I bought and projects I was working on. I'd ask questions about clothing, fashion and make controversial statements to get people talking. I did that every day - I was known for it.

I made some great connections in those days. I can't count the amount of times someone connected with me and said, "My sister's cousin's friend told me about you", or some other lengthy route that connected us.

Start conversations in your area of interest and provide answers.
Be the go-to person in your field.
Be the person others recommend.
Be the resident expert in people's minds!!

How do you stay consistent on social media?

You have to show up every day (I'll cover more of this in chapter 10, Divine Marketing Strategies).

Be consistent and give
visibility to your activity.

For me, one Tuesday morning for example, I had just taken a delivery of stock to the warehouse and I jumped on Facebook and Instagram Live and shared what was happening. To me, this is mundane, normal, basic, everyday work but this is the story behind the brand that people love and buy into.

There are some elements of me that I personally like to keep private, so you won't really see pictures of my children on social media but anything to do with business, connected to business, ministry, training and development, are what I like to share.

The less you post the less
of a pulse the business has.
The more you post the more
you keep visibility, exposure and life
pumping to the business.

The biggest thing is visibility. If you can get into a rhythm of posting every day, creating a video or doing a live stream once or twice every week, this is the heartbeat of the business that is pumping visibility to the world, so you can be seen, heard and felt.

How do you keep up social media engagement when you don't feel like it?

There have been many seasons where I've had to keep posting through my pain. Through seasons of discouragement, grief, serious family illness, when I just wanted to shut down for a few weeks or take a couple months off, I had to find something within me (God strength) to keep going. When I did shut down for a few weeks it was definitely reflected in the business income. I lost visibility, people forget quickly in this information-attention-grabbing day.

It's easy to post and be engaging when life is good, when creativity is flowing and you're inspired. Some of the hardest times to post is when I'm uninspired and going though painful personal times. But some of my most engaging social media posts and powerful emails have been when **I posted through my pain**. All I want to do in those times is CHECK OUT and come back when things are better but when I allow God to use that pain, it's powerful.

Posting through your pain makes you transparent, trustworthy and relatable. It's not nice, it's not comfortable but it's potentially where your greatest power lies.

Here is one of my most engaging emails. It was brutally honest. It was hard to send but we actually had an incredible amount of sales that weekend. I sent it to be transparent and forewarn my clients about an upcoming price increase but the business ended up being blessed because of my vulnerability:

Subject: Important message. Just wanted you to know.

29th September 2017

From my desk to your ears

This week we had a really intense business meeting (the presence of God was with us, it was beautiful). In that meeting I had to be honest about some real issues facing the country and had been impacting our business for a while now.

Have you heard about Brexit? The value of our pound dropped dramatically over the last year. This has affected all of our international buying and selling.

After the news of Brexit lots of businesses here in the U.K. closed immediately, most businesses reacted by increasing prices. I, on the other hand, believed it would pass and tried to ride out the storm by absorbing these additional costs. This worked for a while... the pound is gaining some strength but is nothing like it was before June last year.

Most companies wouldn't send a warning but I choose to be transparent and give you the heads up that on Monday 2nd October 2017 we will be increasing our prices.

To serve ministries I've always tried to keep our prices down, (although I've been told time and time again my prices should be at least double for the quality, design and service we offer).

So this week's business meeting was crunch time!

1.   Increase prices and be around for a long time to continue serving the men and women of God

2.   Keep going as we are and ignore the haemorrhaging.

So we've gone with option 1 but not until Monday 2nd October.

If there's something you've been meaning to get for a while this would be a great time to do it.

(Unfortunately we won't be able to take back orders at current prices).

You can purchase what's available in store now in our:

- *Women's Store*

- *Men's Store &*
- *Outlet*

It's an honour to serve you,
Camelle

I remember in October 2014 we were celebrating twenty thousand people on our Facebook page. I received a word in my spirit, "you haven't even scratched the surface". Today we have over one hundred thousand people on our Facebook Page. Remember, this started with me being known for something – fashion design – on my personal profile, to starting a "House of ilona Clergy" Facebook Page from nothing, growing it, 'like' by 'like'.

Since 2014, we have become widely known with tens of thousands of clients and customers worldwide and it still feels like the beginning of something.

MY ADVICE

What's the key advice you'd share with someone pursuing his or her dream?

The main things I have lived by in my entrepreneurial journey are focus, balance and consistency. Listen to your desires and seek God because He has put the desire in your heart.

When God made you, He wrapped your heart in a desire. He has put the desire in you already. The next step is to seek Him for it. Tell Him how much you want to fulfil that desire and then He will give you the desire of your heart (that he put there in the first place).

How did you make the transition from being an employee to an entrepreneur?

I was always an employee-preneur! I went above and beyond on my jobs, from my first job at a hair salon - washing hair and tidying up (I had a queue for customers wanting me to shampoo them), to working for my local council. When my first role there, covering maternity cover, was over, they couldn't let me go, because I went and found all the gaps in the department, created a job description for myself and presented it to them. They couldn't say no, they rehired me and paid me more money!

I was a great employee. That's the place to start. Prosper where you are currently planted, be a blessing. Work as though you're employed by God Himself. Give your absolute best, bring your A-Game. It will be noticed. You also need to prove to yourself you'd be a good employee. Would you employ you? That's ultimately what you're doing when your start your own business. You need to be able to do your best work with no one pushing you but you.

Go above and beyond.
Innovate in your space.
See, work and think
yourself into greater.

As an employee, I had an entrepreneurial mind. I read entrepreneurial books. I was always very driven, doing more than necessary. I was an asset wherever I went (that's what all my employers said). I was working on being a good steward and excited to one day being able to use my skills and assets for the Kingdom of God and direct my potential to the places I felt called to use it.

So, making the transition from employee to entrepreneur was natural, it still had its mind-set challenges. I have to be on, working, pushing and driving all the time. For me, as an employee, in some jobs I had, I could take my foot off the gas, now and then, because I would still get paid. Some jobs, as long as you show up, you'll get paid. As an entrepreneur running my own business, I don't have that luxury (but sometimes it would be nice).

THE FUTURE

What's next for you?

As we now have great business systems in place flowing beautifully, it's freeing up more of my time, so I'm starting to speak a bit more - I've finally had the space to write this book. I am able to do more coaching to help other creatives launch their dreams.

*****

Story Time

I have a real passion for seeing people fulfil their potential and live out their dreams and desires. In this vein, I would now like to introduce my incredible nephew, Devanté, who had a desire to work in the fashion industry. He asked questions, took bold steps, now he's fulfilled as he is living his dream. Here's his story:

> *Christmas 2013... My earliest memory of our first conversation about the fashion industry, I knew my Aunty Cam had her own label and designed her own garments but never spoke in true depth! Around this time, I had decided to switch professions and make my way into the creative industry. Coming from a black middle class family, many members couldn't give me advice because they themselves didn't have the*

experience or know anyone that had the industry knowledge.

Speaking to Aunty was a blessing because she really gave me the keys to unlock a new mind-set and showed me that prayer works! She always said she spoke to God before anything in her work was agreed or decided. I continued to do the same. As a previous graduate of the London College of Fashion, I remember mentioning that once I finish my 2-year fashion college course, it would be my goal to pass and get into the university.

Over the duration of those years, which were a struggle, my aunty would always send words of encouragement and at family functions I would update her with designs I had been working on. She would always be so proud, which would mean so so so much to me!!

Summer 2015 - I passed my course and got accepted into the prestigious University of London College of Fashion! I was so amazed and I remember texting Aunty Cam first telling her the news and my God!! If I ever could screenshot a message and frame it, this would be it! The encouragement and joyful message really came from the heart and her words really spoke life into me and gave me the confidence to continue to be who I AM in Christ and never let anything distract me from the path He has for me.

Present 2019 - I graduated with Upper Second Class honours and have worked for numerous magazines, celebrities and launched my own brand.

AUNTY CAM, honestly you've been such an inspiration to me and a great mentor, the heart you have and time you have to give to me and many others is truly incredible and I really thank God you're in my life and continue to give me advice and wisdom to this day. I pray that you will continue to influence many thousands and millions and continue to be the wonderful and courageous woman God wants you to be.

Love you loads.

Devanté Daley, nephew
Stylist & Fashion Designer
Instagram; @DVNTEXX
Brand Instagram; @ENVISM

I am so proud of my nephew for taking bold steps in the direction he really wanted to go in. He networks, goes for opportunities and isn't afraid to have conversations with key people.

What I love about Devanté is the powerful and specific questions he would ask me every time we met. He knew what I was doing and what advice I could offer him. He recently gave me an incredible compliment - *"Auntie, you give away keys. You just share and people in this industry don't do that!"* I have nothing to fear because all I have comes from God and the more I give away, the more He blesses me with. Don't buy into the scarcity mind-set; our God is abundant and limitless.

Ask yourself the questions in this chapter:

- What's your source of creativity?
- Where is your creative space?
- How do you manage the hard times?
  (Plan this in the good times so the hard times can be easier to manage)
- Where do you need to be more consistent?
- How do you stay motivated?
- Where are you juggling but need to create more balance?
- What does showing up on Social Media look like for you?

Chapter 9
Money matters of the heart

Where your treasure is that's where you'll find your heart. Where do you make, spend and invest your treasure/money? This says more about where your heart is than your words ever could.

What is your motive for the money? What a powerful question! When you picture God blessing you, what is your motive and intention for the abundance? It's so important to take time out to think about how abundance feels to you.

Do you want to get it so you can give it all away? Why? Do you feel you don't deserve it? Does God need to teach you how to give and how to keep?

Do you want to get it and keep it? Why? Because others can't be trusted with your hard-earned wealth? You made it so you deserve to keep it, right?

Our motive towards money says everything about

where our heart is, because where your treasure is (money, that which is precious to you), that's where we'll find your heart.

I'm starting to realise how big the money and heart connection are. How you feel about tithing, giving offering, giving to the poor and those around you in need when it is in the power of your hand to do it, says more about your heart than your lips ever could.

Recently, this has been a recurring theme for me. One Saturday I was on the train with my friend Naomi, heading to London to spend the day in intense Market Place training with The Business Bishop, Bishop Wayne Malcolm. Expectation was high and we got onto the subject of money.

We are in our thirties and homeowners. She's starting a new job next month where she will be making more money. She has already planned to keep her lifestyle at the same level and has assigned her extra income to her mortgage to make over payments. We were sharing nuggets of knowledge for paying off our mortgage in five to ten years. Things like:

- knowing what is the maximum lump sum you can pay each year without paying penalties,
- paying at least half your mortgage payment two weeks early each month can

> reduce the interest you pay, and making regular over payments.

It was a powerful conversation, which led our imaginations to the day, in the not too distant future, where we could say, "We are completely mortgage free!" We had to take a moment and take it in. Then our minds jointly began to dream of what we could do with wealth (the motive for the money). We could see needs in our community and abroad and fund them, just like that. Pay off someone's bills, start a school - the ideas were flowing and it was beautiful.

So much of what we discussed on the train was confirmed by the Business Bishop at the Market Place event that day.

Great financial times

My clergy business has done well financially. The year I followed God's leading to focus on the clergy line, the business income was three times what my last salary was. There were a lot of outgoings but there was enough money being made to pay the business bills and produce more products. Peter, who is incredibly supportive, was happy to take care of the house bills and allowed me to keep reinvesting into the business, which is what I did. I barely took a salary.

The following year the business' annual income

doubled, it was in the five figures and such an incredible achievement. I still was not taking a regular salary. In a way it felt noble. Our garments aren't cheap but they're also not designer prices. I do my best to cater to the clients we serve. Some of our clients have high disposable incomes and others barely have any.

When people would complain about our prices I knew I could justify the cost - "*You're paying for this dress, the associated costs of making, marketing and getting this dress to you, along with paying towards another dress that we can put into production for someone else and to keep the business moving*". If I needed to, if someone pushed me hard enough, in my back pocket, I had, "*I don't even take a salary!*" Yes, sadly I felt justified.

By now, I was paying a full-time salary to our first employee, plus all the other business bills and reinvesting heavily into more stock. Still barely taking a salary myself.

The following year the annual income of the business doubled again. I now had a full-time and part-time employee.

I was travelling on the train, this time on my way to a Business Seminar in Birmingham, reading a scripture about the labour of love. This was often the term I used for what I do in business. But today my prayer is *"Lord this has been a labour of love, you've seen my heart but I need to get paid. I have employees who work hard and get paid, I work hard and should get paid too."* But I still felt guilty.

The speaker at this seminar was a multi-millionaire entrepreneur, who is also a Christian. Some of the areas he spent a long time dealing with were money, mind-set and practical steps to take as a business owner. He said, "If you're getting paid less in your business than you would a job, it's not worth it, quit and go get a job. Why suffer?" OUCH. This hit me so hard!! I wasn't paying myself and it felt noble. I worked so hard, yet couldn't go on that holiday with my friends or sisters. I used the excuse of 'schedule' but really, I knew I could barely afford it because all the business money was for the business and it was going back into the business. I had told myself I couldn't take it for myself and go on *holiday!*

In one of the breaks I got talking to the speaker's wife. She loved my business! I began to share how convicted I was about what her husband said in the last session about taking a salary. She shared that this was something even he struggled with at one point. SHE WENT IN ON ME! She asked me about my role in my business and about all the things I did. Then she asked me this,

"If you brought someone into your company on an executive level to do all the things you do, would you pay them?"

"Of course I would!" I replied in shock. "I take care of my people..."

Interrupting me, she added, "Then why are you treating your current CEO like that?"

I was stunned! I didn't see it like that. I knew things had to change.

Outsourcing and downsizing

I went from making garments to order, to having manufacturers produce everything for me.

I went from picking and packing orders myself in the spare room of our home, to employing staff who would pick and pack orders from the stock shelves of my rented office space - located under a church building, might I add.

We had around one thousand units of stock in the office, a full-time and a part-time member of staff. The staff were spending pretty much all of their time doing fulfilment (picking and packing orders), leaving me to run the business, marketing and customer service. Growing the business would mean expanding the range, a bigger office space for more stock and staff.

I spoke to a Business Strategist about the business and he said, "Your business model is excellent, but you're spending too much time on fulfilment - outsource it!"

I had known about Fulfilment Companies years earlier, but at that time I wasn't ready to hand all my precious products to a company to handle. But it was a few years on and I was already one step removed, as I wasn't handling fulfilment of the products anymore, staff were doing this for me. So the next natural step was a fulfilment company. They would get much better shipping rates, storage would be limitless and now I could really grow and expand the business.

It made sense, it was the natural progression and it was time. After praying and weighing everything up with Peter and my Fashion Business Consultant, we made the decision to outsource fulfilment.

I found a local company right away. Peter and I met with them and it was a seamless process. All hands were on deck, everything got boxed up and labelled. The shelving and stock were gone. (I actually took a picture of the back of the delivery guy as he took away my last boxes of stock). It was both sad and exhilarating - mourning that part of the business and excited about the future potential.

After this, we had a team meeting to discuss the skill set everyone could bring to the company now that fulfilment wasn't the main activity. It felt like a new business. We could put some energy behind ideas we previously didn't have time to focus on.

Things were also tight financially so we needed some big ideas to drive things forward. It's tough working for a small business. Sometimes, you have to get in, and do a bit of everything. I have such an entrepreneurial mind - if I was a staff member in a company which was shifting focus and really wanted to stay with the company, I would be fighting for my seat at the table. I'd bring my best ideas, show the value I bring and why the company could not afford to lose me! Am I saying that because it's my business? Am I saying that because that's the energy I bring everyday anyway?

Having to let go of these staff members, who were also my friends was one of the hardest things I have ever done. They had helped me grow. But the business had changed, I couldn't keep paying them for their previous role and it wasn't clear exactly what this new world looked like. Neither were they sure what they could offer. It was hard, very hard, but a necessary step in this season of change.

Transition

I'm sitting in this massive office space on my own, but not alone. It feels massive. Once there were one thousand clergy dresses, blouses, stock and two other people working - now it's just me.

What I missed the most was the conversations my staff and I had, my best ideas would come mid-sentence. Who would I bounce my ideas off of now?

That's when I heard *"speak to me!"*

This is when I began to have meetings with God, where I would go into some epic times of speaking with Him in meetings; the ideas and perspectives on things were quite literally, out of this world. Other times I would just flow with God in my work. As ideas came, I would execute them, then flow into something else, then something else. Then the alarm would sound to pick up my girls from school and it was like coming out of a cloud.

I remember speaking to my sister, Kimberley, about some pictures I needed for the business. I didn't know what I needed; I just knew I needed pictures. I sounded so unclear when I was speaking to her.

I heard *"ask me."* So, I said I would call her back.

I hung up, prayed and asked God, "What pictures do I need for this business?" I grabbed a notebook and pen, ready for an answer. I felt the urge quite strongly, to write the numbers 1 to 10 down the side of the page and then my mind was flooded with ideas. I wrote ferociously. A few minutes later I called my sister back with an entire photo schedule for the year. We were both blown away. Thank you Lord.

Finding Divine Flow

This is how I find my Divine Flow. I bring God in intentionally. I'll ask Him in the morning, "What do I post on my social media? What do I say on Facebook Live or in an email to my list?" Sometimes I get the answer right away, other times I get the inspiration right when I need it and I do my best to remember to give God thanks.

When my heart, business, motive and intentions are surrendered to God, business is effortless. When my heart is surrendered and my affections are set on God the business grows! Someone mentions the company on a Facebook Page that I don't know about, and we suddenly get an influx of orders. A church has finally given their Leadership the go-ahead to order their clerical attire for upcoming ordinations and have recommended House of ilona; everyone is keen to get their orders in right away. Business takes a leap.

It's not an exact science,
it's relationship.

Are there times when my heart is fixed but the business is still struggling? Yes.
Are there times when my head and heart are in another place and the business is booming? Yes.
I don't have the exact answers but I try to be aware of the common patterns and themes in my life.

In the past I had really struggled with this. My heart would be fixed on God. Sales start climbing, it excites me and I start to plan for all the new things I can produce with the money and the new stock I can finally get in. My plans get bigger and I need even more money. (Where's my heart now?) I then try to figure out what I did to cause the sales to increase and wonder if I can repeat it. This is where things are slippery! The numbers begin a slow decline.

'And thou say in thine HEART,
My power and the might of
mine hand hath gotten me this wealth.
But thou shalt remember the Lord thy God:
for it is he that giveth thee power to get wealth,
that he may establish his covenant
which he sware unto thy fathers, as it is this day.'
Deuteronomy 8:17-18 KJV

I truly believe your business reflects you:

- When I didn't value the worth of my products neither did other people
- When I began to see and understand the incredible worth and value of my products, so did others
- I have found that my thoughts and feelings are directly reflected in my business
- I find that when my heart is surrendered to God, everything flows beautifully
- When my heart is focused on the money it's a struggle.

On a personal note

I am strong today because of what God has taken me through. Yes I am working hard and making some things happen but that strength I'm using is because God has trained me in the gym of life to be able to do what I'm doing today. My results today are not attributed just to today; these results are from everything that led to today.

Here is my personal, modern day interpretation of Deuteronomy chapter 8:

> *There was a time I almost didn't make it but God kept me in the wilderness of life and fed me when I didn't know where the next meal was coming from.*
> *I could still be in that season now but I made it through.*
> *Now I have a lovely house, food in the fridge and running water.*
> *The danger I face is looking at today, looking at the work I do, the effort I put in and the results it brings. It's so easy to look at that and think it's all me.*
> *Plus, the enemy of my soul whispers lies like "You did it, it's all you!"*
> *"You smashed it!"* (Can you hear the lies?)
>
> *I am careful to remember that it is God that has given me the power to get wealth! Yes,*

there is plenty that I'm doing but I wouldn't even be here without Him!

On a very basic level, it's like saying to a parent, "I got to where I am without you!" You wouldn't even be here without them. How much more our Creator, Saviour and Keeper?

He did all this so you would never say to yourself,
'I have achieved this wealth with
my own strength and energy.'
Remember the LORD your God. He is the one who gives
you power to be successful, in order to fulfill the
covenant he confirmed to your ancestors with an oath.
Deuteronomy 8:17-18 NLT

Treasure and the heart

'For where your treasure is,
there will your heart be also.'
Matthew 6:21 KJV

Where your treasure is there will your heart be also. So, show me where your money is and that will show me exactly where your heart is. Before you even get paid, what have you already spent your money on? Do you take ten per cent of your income and give it back to God? That's a huge megaphone message about where your heart is. No excuses. I know it can be hard when your whole wage sometimes isn't even enough to cover the basics but I'd prefer ninety per cent with God's promised hand of protection than one hundred per cent without it.

If riches increase don't set your heart on them

'If riches increase, set not your heart upon them.'
Psalms 62:10 KJV

If you are blessed to have riches increase in your life, don't set your heart on them. Instead set your affections (emotions, heart and mind) on the things above. It's a matter of the heart.

'Set your affection on things above,
not on things on the earth.'
Colossians 3:2

God is not concerned about you
having money; He's concerned
about money having you.

Money isn't the root of all evil,
it's <u>the love of</u> money that is the root of all evil
1 Timothy 6:10

There is a big heart and money connection. Our heart and love can subtly move from God to money. It's the culture we live in. As Bishop Wayne Malcolm states,
    "We need to focus on the Mission not the money"

Chapter 10
Divine Marketing Strategies

I remember hearing the term "Divine Marketing Strategies" when I was younger and it has stuck with me ever since. I loved God and enjoyed marketing, so this resonated. I would often pray for Divine Marketing Strategies for my work and when helping others.

There are many times I would get into a conversation with someone about their business and their target market and the ideas would just begin to flow out of me like a river. Once this happened at home with Peter, and I had to pause so he could hit 'record' on his phone and the stream of ideas came from deep within me. I was blown away by how it all came together and how simple and tailored it was.

I don't know what it is about marketing, but I just love it. I always have, I love helping people connect. It came naturally to me the more I learnt about marketing in college and in my continued education, where it opened things up even more. I was able to name and categorise the concepts. I understood the essence of it. I love this idea of connecting people to things, speaking their language through words and pictures.

I knew I had to write this chapter because recently I have had three different conversations with people about their marketing and by the end, they were blown away by the actionable, marketing strategies I had given them. It flows out so effortlessly. It's like a puzzle and the pieces are comprised of the product or service and the various people who need them. Is there a direct connection? Or do we need other pieces to connect them both?

*'And Jesus returned in the power of the Spirit into Galilee: and **there went out a fame of him through all the region** round about'*
Luke 4:14 KJV

There was no Facebook, Twitter or Instagram, but after Jesus went through His greatest trial, the fame of Him was spread throughout the region. Now this, is Divine Marketing in action!

The massive shift

Marketing has changed so much. I studied business and marketing from 1995 to 2007 in school, college, then in my studies with the Chartered Institute of

Marketing. We focused mainly on offline marketing (print advertising, face-to-face, radio, TV etc.), which was around eighty to ninety per cent of my studies, with only ten to twenty per cent focus on online marketing (social media, website, blog, search engine etc.).

Skip forward twelve years to today and I found myself running a successful business but I was doing ninety per cent online marketing and ten per cent offline. Even the offline elements are generated online first.

I struggled with this for a few years in business. I understood it was a whole new world of marketing but it was hard to accept that my twelve years of studying offline marketing was in vain. But it wasn't in vain. I was using offline principles online every day. One of the offline principles we were taught was to drip feed information. People need seven contacts or touch points to feel comfortable to buy from you. I wasn't using tools such as billboard, radio, TV, PR, direct mail promotions, vehicle livery, in store displays and point of sale promotions to get all seven touch points as I was taught. My ads would find my ideal clients online and seven touch points could happen all at once, thereby creating an instant sale. A sale would happen within seven days, or simply - yet powerfully - being the company of choice that people would go to when they have the need which we could supply. It may look like this;

Seven touch points for a potential instant sale:

1. Potential client sees our Facebook Ad and it resonates with them
2. They click the Ad
3. They 'like' our page
4. They scroll through and get to know us some more
5. They click the website link and browse the shop
6. They read testimonials
7. They find some garments in their size and they buy.

This actually happens, I have spoken to clients on the phone who just found us on Google or Facebook that day.

Seven touch points for a potential sale in seven to fourteen days:

1. Potential client sees our Facebook Ad and it resonates with them
2. They click the Ad
3. They 'like' our page
4. They scroll through and get to know us some more
5. They click the website link and browse the shop
6. They request a catalogue and receive it in seven days
7. With catalogue in hand they're back on the website to buy.

I have seen names on catalogue requests one week and then names on order boxes the following week.

Seven touch points for being the go-to company for whenever the sale is due to happen:
1. Potential client sees our Facebook Ad and it resonates with them
2. They click the Ad
3. They 'like' our page
4. They scroll through and get to know us some more
5. They click the website link and browse the shop
6. Join our email list
7. They may get one hundred plus more touches via Facebook and emails until they are ready to buy.

We offer FREE next day delivery in the UK and two to three day's international delivery via DHL Express. When this new client is happy with their new garment, the speed of delivery and the overall service, we have a new client who will hopefully come to us first for their needs and recommend us.

So, marketing has changed massively from when I studied it. Now it's very much about your online presence and visibility.

Your feed on Facebook, Twitter and Instagram is the breadcrumbs that give people a taste of you and leads to a deeper level of trust, connection and a sale or recommendation. You cannot put a price on a word of mouth recommendation; it's pretty much a guaranteed connection and sale.

The feed shows your recent history and can go back for years. It gives people a taste and a flavour of your journey and how your story has evolved. The history has your potential client saying, *"You've been at this for a while, I can pay my money because you don't look like the company that has just arrived and might run off with my money and not be here next week. You reply to people, you're present. You might have posted on your story in the last 24hrs which gives me even more comfort and reassurance you can be trusted and contacted."*

When you start to use your Facebook and Instagram stories you now become a living breathing persona behind the company. Within 24hrs the potential client has seen snippets of your day and thoughts. They get to see what you're doing as you bring them into your world and your journey.

Raise visibility of your activity

The classic book by Dale Carnegie, *How To Win Friends And Influence People* outlines in great detail about people wanting to do business with those they know, like and trust. Marketing today is about bringing people into your reality and activities; they want a glimpse behind the scenes. This is the reality show generation. You can't just say, "it's customers first" anymore, people need to feel it and see social proof of it.

Marketing from a place of purpose

I listen to so much business training, learn new strategies, and encounter ideas and suggestions from clients and colleagues, that it's important for me to go back to my original intent often. I need to figure out where these new concepts and ideas fit in.

I have to go back to the place where I first fell in love with the idea, back to the place of joy and excitement. What is it all about?

Our clients are women who are great dressers with an incredible wardrobe and sense of style. Before House of Ilona, when our client needed to wear a collar, she would be in a shapeless shirt (possibly her husband's old shirt) that didn't reflect her look, style and character. I wanted to create a look that reflected her style.

> Our business strap line is:
> *Helping women look good*
> *on the outside is our business,*
> *Helping women feel good*
> *on the inside is our heart.*

This always brings me back to the original intent. This is the feeling the garments and the marketing produce. Designing great clergy garments and matching that with an excellent service enables the women of God to look good on the outside. A lot of our marketing is encouragement and inspiration to uplift and inspire, so these women of God can also feel good on the inside.

I'll often do a Facebook Live on a Monday. If the women of God have been preaching and ministering on the weekend, Monday is usually the day to rest and recoup, so we send out encouragement and sometimes even pray on Facebook Live on a Monday. I will pray that God would restore what they poured out back into them.

These tailored, targeted actions have come through years of studying our clients; who they are, what they need and figuring out how we can fulfil the mission of making them look good on the outside and feel good on the inside. There is so much more work to do in both these areas, I am enjoying the process.

Women have said things like:
"Wearing House of ilona Clergy makes me feel good in my collar"
"I feel authentically me"
"I was excited about the call of God on my life but I was most concerned about what I would wear, I still wanted to look like and feel like me. So, thank you for

this clergy line"
"Where have you been for the last 30 years of my ministry?"
"I would just wear my husband's old clergy shirt with a jacket"
"Now I can Minister and feel like a Lady".

Find them

Find your ideal client,
get to the know them, serve them
and build relationship.

My product is: clergy clothing for women

My target market is: women in Ministry, women of the cloth

My message is delivered in their language; the language of Ministry and the love of God. I speak this through my marketing. These are women who give and give and give some more. They are always on duty, having just completed one assignment and preparing for another, any minute the phone could ring and it could be any type of news with a new demand on their time. I understand this and tailor my message to be uplifting and encouraging. The emails they open from us are about giving and blessing, not taking and demanding.

They are the ones always speaking, giving and pouring into others, so it's a blessing to be able to give back and pour into them. When I can tap into these needs, that's where the power of my marketing lies.

It's taken me years of trial and error, listening to feedback and prayerful reflection to get here and I'm still learning.

The types of marketing I do are:
- Social Media
- Emails
- Catalogue Requests
- Thank you cards.

All these revolve around our strapline of helping women look good on the outside and feel good on the inside.

Marketing is Exposure

Exposure to those who know you, reminding them of who you are and what you can do for them. It is also about raising the awareness of who you are and what you offer to those who don't know you.

Top Tips:

What your thinking should be before you start your marketing activities:

- Go back to the original intention and reconnect with your mission
- Think about what the client needs and seek to serve
- Speak their language, use their words, tone and phrasing
- Be ready to raise the visibility of your activities. Be seen, felt and earn trust through your social feeds and in your stories.

Chapter 11
Developing Your Personal Style

We've explored purpose,
what does that look like in terms of style?

Please note, I am writing from the perspective of a Fashion designer and not a stylist. I now wish to talk about Finding your Divine Flow *in the context of* your style. You need to be able to connect your style with your purpose so when you arrive in your Godfidence you need to show up and make a statement without saying a word, through how you present yourself.

Styling on purpose

Who are you? What do you do? Where are you going in life and what does that look like?

There is a poster on the inside of my wardrobe:

Dress how you want to be addressed.
Dress like who you want to dress.

So, every time I put my outfits together I'm reminded. I start to remove the things that don't look like how I want to look and slowly add the things that look like how I want to look.

How do you want to be addressed?
I want to be addressed as The Photographer.
I want to be addressed as The Artist.
I want to be addressed as The Designer.
I want to be addressed as The ...... (Fill in the blank for yourself).

This chapter is on Develop***ing*** your Personal Style. Just like the title of this book is Find***ing*** Divine Flow, the reason these words are 'developing' and 'finding' is because the 'ing' makes it an on-going process. Even when you hit the mark and you master your look and style, embrace it, but don't be surprised when things change. Life changes, circumstances change, the seasons change and our body shape changes. You may have a change in taste or direction.

There are constantly changes going on within and around you, so even when you nail it this summer, how does that translate to the autumn/winter season?

Process your look and style

Take some time to journal and think about your 'why'. Why do you wear what you wear? Also process why you don't wear what you want to wear.

- Is it because somebody said something when you were younger or could it be more recent?
- Was there once an off-handed comment that stayed with you?
- Is it because of how someone else looked in something?

As a designer, I love certain styles, I would see something "that looks amazing!" Then I would go and make the same outfit for myself and it didn't look amazing on me. I had to learn that there was a reason certain outfits look great on certain people. It is not necessarily the outfit itself, as some looks can't be recreated – instead a number of factors come into play, such as the personality, body shape and the general mood of the person wearing the outfit. So many more things aligned to make the moment great, not just the outfit they were wearing.

"The kind of beauty I want is the hard-to-get kind that comes from within – Strength, Courage, Dignity."
Ruby Dee

I've learnt to see someone and say "that looks absolutely amazing, ON THEM!"

When walking around the shops with Peter I have to be specific (in case he wants to surprise me later) "great outfit, not for me though", or, "I would definitely wear this, this has my name all over it!!"

Know yourself and process your own style.

"The joy of style lies not in how we look to other people, but in how we look to ourselves - and the most memorable and beautiful outfits are simply those that, in some rare moment of joy, we find the courage to share with the world."
Simon Van Booy

Be ready for your moment

Have your outfit ready for that opportunity you're waiting on. Go and get THAT dress, so when the opportunity knocks, you don't have to run to the shops, but you're ready! It's in the wardrobe with the tag on. I don't mean having a wardrobe full of brand new things with tags on, I just mean one or two pieces for THAT special occasion; those shoes that stay in the box so when that opportunity comes you're ready.

Be courageous

Do you have the courage to dress out loud?
To dress the way you REALLY want to?

"Beauty begins the moment you decide to be yourself."
Coco Chanel

Take courage in your style. Be courageous. Be bold. Be different. Do you always wear black because you once heard that black was flattering or maybe you were in a season of mourning? But it's twenty years later and you're still wearing all black, all the time. Take small steps like getting some brighter jewellery, some tops to brighten up your wardrobe and your life.

"Style is having the courage of one's choices
and the courage to say no. It's good taste and culture."
Giorgio Armani

Take some courageous steps, go shopping and try on some things that you think would never suit you. Be bold enough to try. That style you see in your head that represents you and where you're going - it takes courage to step into it.

"Dress shabbily and they remember the dress.
Dress impeccably and they remember the woman."
Coco Chanel

It takes courage
- to get rid of some things that you've been holding on to for years; for whatever reason
- to clear out two-thirds of your wardrobe because you know that you don't wear any of

that stuff and you're just holding onto it because maybe "one day it will fit me", "it might come back into fashion" because, because, because

- to admit that you only wear one third of your wardrobe and if you remove the old you make space for the new.

"You call me out beyond the shore into the waves. You make me brave."
Amanda Cook – Lyrics: Bethel Music

The trendsetter of the group

Maybe you look great in what you wear!! Let's take a minute to talk about that Joseph and Esther effect!

Are you the one who just looks amazing in everything you wear? You know how to dress your body and put things together and when you step out you always get compliments. Even when you drag something on to run out, you still get compliments.

People say you just look amazing in everything you put together. That can also have a flip side. You know that jealous, envious spirit when someone says something with their mouth but your spirit picks up their non-verbal communication and if feels 'off'. People can be jealous of what you put together, how you look. What effect does that have on you? Are you resilient or does it make you second guess yourself when you're getting dressed?

Be conscious of any thought, thing or person who consciously or subconsciously makes you want to shrink back on the full expression of yourself!!

One of the best cards I've ever received had a picture of a Disney Princess on the front, in her full royal regalia and it read: *"There's no such thing as over dressed"*. I love that card but it could have been received in two ways:

- Camelle, you're always overdressed. What's wrong with you? OR
- Camelle, you're always overdressed. Wow!

I remember a crisp autumn day where my schedule consisted of going to the office and doing the school run. I had on a cute dusty pink jumper, the right jeans and then I had the pink boots to match and then paused... are the pink boots too much? It finished the outfit off perfectly but I had a reservation. Then I had to liberate myself! *"You know what Camelle, this is you! You are a Fashion Designer. You're a creative entrepreneur, born to stand out not blend in. Don't put on the black shoes put on your pink boots and work your style!"* I had to free myself. It was liberating because it wasn't about who I was going to see or be seen by, but it was about how my outfit would make me feel.

What I wear affects how I feel when I'm sitting at my desk and writing that email. I can shine brighter on that Facebook Live because I got dressed and stepped out on purpose.

Getting dressed and putting on THAT outfit can lift your mood and put you in character. You're not faking it but sometimes you need a little help to step up, because life happens.

Getting dressed up can be great medicine.

Having Godfidence.

This is huge in terms of your personal style because that's the greatest thing you can wear.

"The most beautiful thing you can wear is confidence"
Coco Chanel

**"The most beautiful thing you
can wear is Godfidence"**
Camelle ilona Daley

Let's do some work

The next page has some space for you to think about and complete a style statement. Think about what people say about your look and style and what you would want people to say about your look and style.

People say my look is:

_____

What I want my look to say about me:

_____

In the context of your work, business and or purpose, think about your motive, intention, and look:
Who am I dressing for and why?

_____

What message am I delivering?

_____

My look summed up in three powerful words is;
1. _____
2. _____
3. _____

Now turn the above into a Style Statement;
I Am:

_____

My personal style is:

_____

When I go to _____
and am in the company of_____
without saying a word, the statement I make is

_____

Researching and picking this season's trends

Whether it's Spring/Summer or Autumn/Winter, the magazines are filled with the new season's styles, prints, patterns, colours and trims. Do your research each season. If we're coming into Autumn/Winter 2019/20 for example, do your online research and get familiar with the season's trends.

Once you have the highlights, pick out the trends you already have, the trends that work for you and the trends you would like to try. Now build this into your capsule wardrobe.

Capsule wardrobe

There is so much power in taking the time to plan your style for the season. Habakkuk 2:2 talks about writing a vision and making it plain, and this is a principle that I use. I did this last winter, it was the tail end of summer and we were approaching

September. I did my research and I took some time out to plan a capsule wardrobe and write a vision for what I wanted my look to be that winter.

I wrote it out on a page of A4 in my notebook and didn't look at it again. By December, I came across this page I wrote and as I read it, I was literally describing exactly what I had been dressing like over the previous months. Writing the vision is POWERFUL.

From your season research, think about what you have and what you need from the list below. For example, decide how many jackets you need and in which styles, colours and prints. Think about what you already have that fits and what you need to add. Visualise your look and consider each category.

There's no need to shop for a whole new wardrobe for the new season (but if you can, enjoy). Focus on adding highlights and buying quality staples that will last.

> *"Real style is based on a bankable wardrobe."*
> Mikki Taylor

Core items to consider for your capsule wardrobe this season:

- Jackets
- Tops & Dresses
- Trousers, Jeans, Skirts

- Accessories

Wardrobe organisation

I had done the Marie Kondo method two years ago, but my wardrobe needed a mini overhaul. I had been putting it off, then the thought came to me, I believe it was a simple God idea – 'create a pile':

1. Put away winter/summer clothes
2. Give away to others and to charity
3. Style what's left.

This was simple, powerful and very quick. I did 1 and 2 really fast then number 3 was fun. I took what was left and laid them on my bed then started to create outfits. Because I had everything laid out on the bed it gave me a new perspective of my clothes and I was able to connect and style things I wouldn't usually put together. I placed these styled outfits back in the wardrobe together. Every day for the next two weeks, Peter would ask if it was a new outfit I was wearing. It was the same clothes; I was just wearing them differently. It was like having a whole new wardrobe. I wanted to share this simple wardrobe organising style tip with you.

"The most beautiful thing you can wear is Godfidence"
Camelle ilona Daley

Chapter 12
In the Flow

I hope you have enjoyed reading Finding Divine Flow, my entrepreneurial journey. I wanted to share some of the lessons I've learnt and how I flow with God in business.

I have had some real internal and pivotal moments in this journey; transformational shifts in root issues, divine counseling whilst learning to hear God's voice. I've learnt to not give up but get into God's Divine Flow to fulfil His purpose. I pray that after reading the book, you will never be the same.

I struggled with acceptance

I remember listening to a preacher online and he was explaining that the fruit you see in your life, good or bad, stems from a root. When you deal with the bad root, you'll produce better fruit. He listed examples of bad roots that produced specific fruit. Straight away I prayed: *"Lord what is the bad root in my life producing bad fruit…"* before I could finish, I heard the word "Acceptance". It made me think, because it wasn't like the root and fruit the preacher was listing. Then my whole life flashed before me in pictures:

- First, my parents got married young, had a son and a daughter (most would call this the perfect set). Then nine years later I came along as a surprise to them (but not to God). I always felt left out - by the time I was five, my siblings were teenagers and getting on with their lives.
- I was always sent away during the school holidays to family and godparents. I wasn't home because my parents were working and I was with other families and felt like the odd one out.
- In school, I was a Christian and unashamed but that came with a backlash too – even though on the last day of school those hardest on me had the most respect for me and what I stood for.

I could go on and on. There was a theme of being different from everyone else, standing out and generally not being accepted.

With this knowledge, every day I would look in the mirror and declare, "I Am Accepted in the Beloved" (Ephesians 1:6). No matter who did or did not accept me, or who accepted me today and didn't the next.

There was one place I was ALWAYS Accepted and that was in God.

Identifying and addressing this root, producing bad fruit in my life, was life changing.

Money Focus Versus Mission Focus

When I focus on the money, it's a struggle, it's never enough and I'm always reaching for more. When I focus on the mission, the money flows effortlessly. For years I have had to make a huge effort to keep my focus on the mission. It's so easy to focus on the money because it's measurable. I always keep in mind to:

Be engaged in the process but stay emotionally detached from the outcome.

The Wonderful Counsellor

One day I watched a powerful counselling session on TV, it was so well done. We literally saw this lady go through the stages, from shock, denial, anger, bargaining, depression, testing, to acceptance.

I am always seeking purpose and to better myself, so I said, "I think I need a counsellor, I want to figure things out and have a breakthrough like that!" So, before I went looking up local Christian counsellors, an old Clarke Sisters' song came to mind, "He's a Wonderful Counsellor..." and that night I prayed "God, counsel me!" I waited, and nothing, so I went to bed.

The next day, so many things happened. Three of four things made me cry - I had breakthroughs in a few areas of my life, a fuller understanding of why certain people interacted with me the way they did. I spoke to my sister about it and said, "I don't know what's happening today, I've just been in pieces and..." then it hit me, "Oh my gosh! The Lord answered my prayer and has been counselling me all day long!" I gave God thanks for it. It was so well executed, I didn't even realise He was answering me. I am forever changed.

Hearing God's voice

Clear time and space, worship, pray and LISTEN!

I loved hearing a fellow Christian entrepreneur talk about how she has coffee with God in the morning, with her journal. I could picture it and feel it. The next morning, I had my coffee and sat with my journal. I had such an encounter with God, He spoke and spoke and spoke. I wrote everything I heard, through tears I wrote and wrote. He confirmed things, showed me the reason why certain things were happening and spoke into my future. I have never been the same.

Do I do this every day? One day my answer will be: "Yes, who wouldn't when you have an encounter like that! This is me, every morning!! It's Heaven on Earth. Glorious!"

My real answer at this point in time, is, sometimes. I wish it were every day. I know God shows up every day but I'm not always that reliable. Sometimes I make excuses, there are many to choose from. Other times, if I'm honest, it's the fear of the greatness I see in me through His eyes.

When times are hard I find it easier to keep my heart fixed on Jesus. It's all I've ever known, but as I dare to step into my greatness and the struggle is over, I now need to learn to seek and see God in the soar.

Prayer

Lord let me be the incredibly successful entrepreneur who always has her heart fixed on the things above. Let me always serve God and not money. Let it be me serving you and money serving me, enabling me to do your work. In Jesus name. Amen

Final Words

If you know you're walking in your purpose and doing what you're supposed to be doing... Please don't quit!

> *'So let's not get tired of doing what is good.*
> *AT JUST THE RIGHT TIME we will reap a harvest of*
> *blessing if we don't give up.'*
> Galatians 6:9 NLT

Don't stop three-foot short of gold! In his all-time classic book, *Think and Grow Rich*, Napoleon Hill tells the story of R. U. Harby.

Harby's uncle had gold fever, so he staked his claim and started digging. After a lot of hard work, the uncle found a vein of ore, so he covered up his find and returned home to raise the money for the machinery that he would need to bring the ore to the surface.

They raised the money and Harby travelled with his uncle back to the site to make their fortune. Things started well and before long, they had enough to clear their debts. They were excited, everything from here on would be profit and things were looking good.

Then the supply of gold stopped. The vein of ore had disappeared. They kept on digging, but found nothing. After a while, they quit in frustration and sold their machinery to a junk man for a few hundred dollars.

After they went home in disappointment, the astute junk man called in a mining engineer who checked the mine and calculated that there was a vein of gold just three feet from where Harby and his uncle had stopped digging. The junk man went on to make millions from the mine.

Harby returned home, paid back everyone who had lent him money and was determined to learn from his mistake in giving up too soon. He went on to become a phenomenally successful insurance salesman, more than recouping what he would have made from the gold mine.

He learned the lesson that you need to persevere through difficulties and stay focused if you are to become successful. Whenever you feel like giving up on your dream, remember that you may be just three feet from gold!

What's your purpose and mission statement, what's your 'Why'? The Purpose, Mission and 'Why' are always for the greater good of people.

Currently my Purpose statement is (it will evolve as I do):

Helping Christian Creatives Launch Dreams.

The 'How' is the incremental steps we take to get there. It is via this book, blogs, social media platforms, podcasts, books, programs, one-to-one coaching, speaking and preaching.

Imagine if that Purpose, Mission, 'Why' were not fulfilled? In Esther's case it was a life or death situation for her people. Could someone's destiny be dependent on you fulfilling your purpose?

What if someone connected to me is about to do something world changing and they don't even know it because they're thinking, "Oh it's only a beauty product." What if Esther had said, "All I have to offer is my beauty"? It's her beauty that God used to save her nation. Or, you could say, "Who, me? I have nothing, just…" What's your 'just'? For the woman in 1 Kings 17:12, all she had was some flour and oil. She was ready to eat her last meal and die. But hers and her children's lives were saved, she became debt free and had a reason to live again because she obeyed a word and used what she had.

Your unique anointing is needed!!

You have been called to the Kingdom, called to your industry, called to your people and tribe for such a time as this.

*Get into God's Divine Flow,
you will fulfil the purpose in you and
you will never be the same.*

REFERENCES

Armani, Giorgio
https://www.azquotes.com/quote/1070022

Barratt, Bianca (December 2018) -
https://www.standard.co.uk/shopping/esbest/fashion-beauty/covent-garden-shopping-guide-a3992006.html

Carnegie, Dale (Vermilion 2006) - How to Win Friends and Influence People,

Cook, Amanda (April 2014) – You Make Me Brave (Lyrics): Bethel Music

Gladwell, Malcolm (Penguin 2009) - Outliers: The Story of Success

Gould, Hallie (July 2014) -
https://www.marieclaire.com/fashion/news/a9366/coco-chanel-quotes/

Hill, Napolean (Vermilion 2004) - Think And Grow Rich

Kondo, Marie (Vermilion 2014) - The Life-Changing Magic of Tidying: A simple, effective way to banish clutter forever

Moran, Brian P & Lennington, Michael (John Wiley & Sons 2013) - The 12 Week Year: Get More Done in 12 Weeks than Others Do in 12 Months

Savelle Foy, Terri (Terri Savelle Foy Ministries 2016) - Dream It. Pin It. Live It.: Make Vision Boards Work for You Audible.co.uk Release Date: 21 July 2016

Taylor, Mikki (Atria Books 2018) - Editor in Chic: How to Style and Be Your Most Empowered Self

Young, Sarah (Thomas Nelson 2004) - Jesus Calling: Enjoying Peace in His Presence

APPENDICES

Appendix 1

Coaching with Camelle

Following on from this book I will produce an online Finding Divine Coaching Program for serious Creatives ready to launch their dreams. I'm not a counsellor, I am a Coach, ready to blow the whistle on procrastination and pull you from where you are to where you are destined to be. It's not pretty, it's intense, it's hard, it can get ugly but it's so worth it!

The Finding Divine Flow Coaching Program is not for everyone. But if you feel you're ready to say yes to You and need a Coach to get you over the line, I would be honoured to work with you. Come here for more information on the program and let's connect:

www.CamelleDaley.com/Coaching

Appendix 2

Kimberley Lawson, Sister
Photographer, Kica Photography
Instagram; @kica_photography

Andrea Louise Francis, friend
Singer Songwriter
Instagram; @ms_andrealouise

Devante Daley, nephew
Stylist & Fashion Designer
Instagram; @DVNTEXX
Brand Instagram; @ENVISM

ABOUT THE AUTHOR

Camelle ilona Daley, CEO of House of ilona. Businesswoman, entrepreneur, speaker, author, business coach and Christian creative. More importantly, wife and proud mother of two beautiful daughters. Camelle lives in Milton Keynes, England where she started the business. *Finding Divine Flow* is her first published work and the culmination of ten plus years in the Fashion Business.

 @CamelleDaley

 @CamelleDaleyLive

 @CamelleDaley

www.CamelleDaley.com

www.Houseofilona.com

www.FindingDivineFlow.com

DO YOU
HAVE
A HANDBAG
YOU NO
LONGER
USE?

FILL IT WITH SNACKS, SANITARY AND

HYGIENE PRODUCTS. NEXT TIME

YOU SEE A HOMELESS

WOMAN GIVE IT TO HER.

add
A LOVELY CARD
and share hope

Printed in Great Britain
by Amazon

10209231R00119